COMMANDERS AND HEROES OF WWII

ROBERT JACKSON

Airlife

Copyright © The Crowood Press Ltd 2003

Written by Robert Jackson

First published in the UK in 2003 by
Airlife Publishing, an imprint of The Crowood Press Ltd

British Library Cataloguing-in-Publication Data
  A catalogue record for this book
  is available from the British Library.

ISBN 1 84037 413 6

Printed in Hong Kong

Airlife Publishing

An imprint of The Crowood Press Ltd
Ramsbury, Marlborough
Wiltshire, SN8 2HR

www.crowood.com

Contents

Field Marshal Viscount Alanbrooke of Brookeborough British Army

Field Marshal Alexander oversaw the campaigns that brought victory to the Allies in the Mediterranean Theatre

Alan Francis Brooke was born in 1883 at Bagnères-de-Bigorre, France, the son of Sir Victor Brooke of County Fermanagh, Northern Ireland. He was educated abroad and then entered the Royal Military College at Woolwich, being commissioned into the Royal Field Artillery in 1902. In 1914 he went to France with the Secunderabad Cavalry Brigade, and in 1915 he became brigade major, Royal Artillery. A succession of staff posts culminated in his appointment, in 1935, as Inspector of the Royal Artillery. In 1936–7 he was Director of Military Training at the War Office, this being followed by his appointment to command the Mobile Division in 1937. In 1939 he was General Officer Commanding-in-Chief, Anti-Aircraft Command, and in 1939–40 he was appointed to command the British Expeditionary Force's II Corps in France.

His next appointment, after the evacuation of British forces from France and the Low Countries, was a supremely important one: he was given command of the British Home Forces, his task being to repel the expected German invasion. From 1941 to 1946 he was Chief of the Imperial General Staff, being made a field marshal in 1944. He was one of the greatest military intellects of his generation, and his grasp of strategic matters was profound; his advice was almost always accepted by the Allied commanders. After the war he was Master Gunner of St James's Park from 1946 to 1956, and from 1950 to 1957 he was Lord Lieutenant of the County of London, a period that also saw his appointment as Constable of the Tower of London (1950–55).

In the post-war years, the publication of Alanbrooke's World War II diaries, *The Turn of the Tide* and *Triumph in the West*, caused a major scandal because of their criticism of the British Prime Minister, Winston Churchill, who was accused of having many failings. There is no doubt, however, that Alanbrooke was correct in his cool appraisal of how the war should be conducted, and he was instrumental in persuading both Churchill and Britain's American allies that to launch a second front prematurely would lead to disaster. The landing at Dieppe in August 1942 proved him right.

Viscount Alanbrooke died in 1963.

Field Marshal Earl Alexander of Tunis
British Army

Destined to become one of the most famous of all British military commanders, Field Marshal Sir Harold Rupert Leofric George Alexander, 1st Earl Alexander of Tunis, was born in 1891 of Anglo-Irish descent. He served in the Irish Guards during World War I, and in the years between 1934 and 1938 he saw service on the turbulent North-West Frontier of India, constantly plagued by rebellious Afghan tribes. The beginning of World War II found him in command of the 1st Division of the British Expeditionary Force in France, when he was responsible for directing the division's brilliant fighting retreat through Flanders. He was in overall charge of the Dunkirk evacuation of May–June 1940, and in 1942 took part in the British Army's long retreat through Burma to the Indian frontier.

From August 1942 he was in command of the Allied forces in the Middle East, overseeing the victorious campaign that resulted in the expulsion of Axis forces from North Africa. He subsequently directed the invasion of Sicily in July 1943 and the bitter fighting that developed after the Allies landed in Italy. In the last year of the European war, appointed to the ultimate British Army rank of field marshal, he was Supreme Allied Commander, Mediterranean, a period that saw sustained strategic successes as German forces in Italy were driven north and finally forced to surrender following a brilliant envelopment at the foot of the Alps. He formulated a plan to strike north towards the Austrian capital, Vienna, but this was overruled by higher authority; however, he succeeded in establishing Trieste as a major Allied command centre in the last days of the war.

Unlike many other great commanders, Alexander never sought the limelight, and his considerable exploits tended to be overshadowed by those of his contemporaries, notably Field Marshal Bernard Montgomery. In 1946 he was appointed Governor-General of Canada, a post he held until 1952, and was created viscount. He served as Minister of Defence under the Conservative administration of Winston Churchill in 1951, and in 1952 was raised to the title of earl. He died in 1969.

Alanbrooke was one of the greatest military strategists of his era, and was openly critical of Prime Minister Winstron Churchill

General Wladyslaw Anders
Polish Army

Born in 1892, General Wladyslaw Anders was in command of the Nowogrodska Cavalry Brigade when Germany invaded Poland in September 1939. On 17 September the Russians also entered Poland from the east, and Anders went into captivity, together with other high-ranking Polish officers. Escaping the fate of thousands of other Polish officers, who were massacred by the Russians, Anders nevertheless endured a hard time in Russian hands, being confined under rigorous conditions and subjected to not infrequent beatings. The situation changed dramatically after 22 June 1941, when the Germans attacked the Soviet Union; Anders and other senior officers were released, well treated and given high commands in the Polish forces which the Soviets were raising to fight the German invaders. In March–August 1942 some 114,000 Polish soldiers and civilians were forcibly deported from camps in the Soviet Union to Persia (Iran), and from these Anders formed the 5th Division, about 5,000 strong. During the lengthy period of rest and recuperation that followed the Poles' ordeal at the hands of the Russians, this was expanded into the Polish Army of the East, which underwent rigorous training and military reorganization following its rehabilitation period.

For operations in Italy, the II Polish Corps was formed, comprising the 3rd Carpathian Rifles Division, the 5th Kresowa Infantry Division, the 2nd Armoured Brigade, Army Group Artillery and support units, including the Polish Women's Auxiliary Service. Under the command of General Anders, II Corps landed in Italy during December 1943 and January 1944 and, as part of the British Eighth Army, took up defensive positions along the Sangro. Earlier, the Polish Commando Company had been sent to Italy for special operations. The Corps' combat route took it to the fourth Battle of Monte Cassino (11–18 May 1944), in which it particularly distinguished itself and played a major part in the capture of Monastery Hill, opening the road to Rome for the Allied forces. In June 1944 the Battle of Ancona led to the capture of this important port by the Polish Corps. Further operations saw the Corps advancing along the Adriatic coast towards Pesaro before moving inland to cover the Eighth Army's flank in the Emilian Apennines. In January 1945 the Corps reached the river Senio, beginning three months of static warfare in preparation for the assault on Bologna, which was captured on 21 April in II Corps' last action. By this time General Anders, who was now C-in-C Polish Forces in the West, had 75,581 fighting troops under his command, a figure that rose to 112,000 by the end of 1945. The vast bulk of these came to Britain as part of the Polish post-war resettlement scheme.

This very able and talented Polish commander died in 1970.

General Anders (seated on the right) confers with British officers during the Italian campaign, 1944. (via J. R. Cavanagh)

Generaloberst Hans-Jürgen von Arnim
German Army

Although an able soldier, von Arnim was left with an impossible task in Tunisia. (Bundesarchiv)

Hans-Jürgen von Arnim was born on 4 April 1889 in Ernsdorf, Reichenbech, Silesia. As the son of General Sixt von Arnim, it was hardly surprising that a Prussian military career was mapped out for him from the moment he first drew breath. In May 1908 he joined the 4th Guards Infantry Regiment as an officer cadet, and by October 1913, as a Leutnant, he was its adjutant. In August 1914 he was assigned as adjutant to the 93rd Reserve Infantry Regiment, with which he was to spend most of World War I. In 1917, by which time he had been wounded twice, he was transferred to the staff of the 4th Infantry Division as ordnance officer, returning to his 93rd Regiment at the end of the year. Post war, he served as a staff officer in various capacities with the Reichswehr, and with the reorganization of the German Army in 1934 he was appointed to command the 1st Battalion of the 2nd Infantry Regiment as an Oberstleutnant. From 1935 to 1938, as an Oberst, he commanded the 68th Infantry Regiment. By December 1939, when he was given command of the 52nd Infantry Division, he was a Generalleutnant.

By the autumn of 1942 von Arnim had risen to command the XXXIX Panzer Corps in Russia, but within a month of the Allied landings in North Africa he found himself at short notice in command of 5th Panzer Army, forming a defensive bulwark in Tunisia. It was von Arnim who succeeded Rommel as commander of Army Group Africa, his orders being to conduct a fighting retreat from the Mareth Line, to plug any dangerous gaps in the Axis defences and to fight off every Allied assault with the utmost ferocity until he no longer had any resources left.

The end was not long in coming. With total air superiority in the hands of the Allied air forces, all attempts to fly supplies and reinforcements into Tunisia met with disaster. On 12 May 1943 the last German resistance collapsed, and Generaloberst Hans-Jürgen von Arnim went into captivity. He was released in 1947, and died at Bad Wildungen on 1 September 1962.

General Henry H. Arnold
US Army Air Force

A formidable organizer, General Arnold was very much a 'hands on' commander, making numerous tours of USAAF establishments overseas. (USAF)

Known universally as 'Hap' throughout his military career, General Henry Harley Arnold was born on 25 June 1886 in Gladwyn, Pennsylvania, and served as Commander of the US Army Air Corps and the US Army Air Forces from 29 September 1938 to 28 February 1946, a period that saw the rise of what was essentially a second-rate air service in the 1930s to become the mightiest and most powerful air force in history.

Graduating from the US Military Academy at West Point on 14 June 1907, Arnold was assigned to the 29th Infantry in the Philippines. On his return to the United States he served at Governor's Island, New York, until April 1911, when he transferred to the Aeronautical Division of the US Signal Corps. On completion of his flight training (in a Wright Flyer) he became a flying instructor at the Signal Corps Aviation School, College Park, Maryland. On 1 June 1912 he established a new altitude record, reaching 6,540 ft (1,995 m) in a Burgess-Wright aircraft. Following another tour in the Philippines (1913–16), he was given the task of organizing a pursuit squadron for the air defence of the Panama Canal Zone. On 30 May 1919 Arnold was appointed Air Officer of the Ninth Corps Area, San Francisco, and exactly a year later he was given the permanent rank of captain. When the US Army Air Corps was formed on 2 July 1926 he was in command of the Air Corps detachment at Marshall Field, Fort Riley,

Kansas. In February 1931 he was promoted to lieutenant-colonel and given command of March Field, Riverside, California. Between 19 July and 20 August 1934, he led a squadron of ten bombers from Washington, DC, to Fairbanks, Alaska, an outstanding feat at that time and one that earned him the Distinguished Flying Cross.

On 11 January 1936 Arnold became Assistant Chief of the USAAC in Washington with the rank of colonel, and on 29 September 1938, as a brigadier-general, he was appointed Chief of the USAAC and Deputy Chief of Staff for Air. The creation of the US Army Air Forces on 20 June 1941 saw him promoted to major-general, and on 9 March 1942 his title was changed to Commanding General, USAAF, in which post he was one of the Joint Chiefs of Staff. On 19 March 1943 Arnold was promoted to the temporary rank of general (four star) and to general of the army (five star) on 21 December 1944. During World War II Arnold made several notable tours of the battlefronts in Europe and the Pacific, being awarded the Distinguished Service Medal for commanding a particularly hazardous 77-hour flight from Bolling Field, DC, to Brisbane, Australia, in 1942.

On 28 February 1946 General Arnold handed over command of the USAAF to his deputy, General Carl Spaatz, and retired from military life to Sonoma County, California, where he died on 15 January 1950.

Field Marshal Sir Claude Auchinleck
British Army

Claude Auchinleck was born in Northern Ireland on 21 July 1884, and educated at Wellington College. He graduated from the Royal Military Academy, Sandhurst, in 1904 and was commissioned into the 62nd Punjab Regiment, seeing action in Egypt, Aden and Mesopotamia. In 1933 he played a key part in overcoming dissident tribes in the North-West Frontier area of India, and in 1938 he was placed in command of the country's Meerut District, with the rank of major-general. On the outbreak of World War II he returned to Britain, and on 7 May 1940 he was given command of the Second Norwegian Expedition, an ill-fated venture from the outset. On 28 May the Allied Expeditionary Force, comprising 25,000 British, French and Polish troops, captured the vital port of Narvik, but when the Germans sent in substantial reinforcements in June Auchinleck was ordered to withdraw.

Promoted to full general, he returned to India as commander-in-chief, but in July 1941 he was appointed C-in-C Middle East in place of General Archibald Wavell. Auchinleck was soon at odds with Winston Churchill, who demanded that he should organize an immediate offensive against Axis forces in North Africa, but Auchinleck insisted on being given time to prepare. Eventually, on 18 November 1941, he launched Operation Crusader, the first offensive of the newly constituted Eighth Army. This was initially successful, raising the siege of Tobruk and recovering Cyrenaica, but early in 1942 Rommel counter-attacked and pushed the British forces back to the Gazala Line. In May–July 1942 he destroyed most of the Eighth Army's armour at the Battle of Gazala and exploited this victory by taking Tobruk, together with 35,000 Allied prisoners, and invading Egypt. Auchinleck assumed personal command of the battered Eighth Army as it withdrew to the Alamein gap; there, he fought Rommel to a standstill in the First Battle of Alamein, and temporarily recovered the initiative by grinding down Rommel's Italian units.

On 8 August 1942, Auchinleck was replaced as C-in-C by General Harold Alexander, with General Bernard Montgomery appointed to command the Eighth Army. Auchinleck had no assignment for almost a year, until he replaced Wavell as C-in-C India on 20 June 1943. He was knighted and made a field marshal in June, 1945, and subsequently had the unenviable task of splitting the Indian Army into the new armies of India and Pakistan. In August 1947 Earl Mountbatten, the last Viceroy of India, compelled Auchinleck to resign on the grounds that he was biased towards the Pakistanis.

Auchinleck left India before Independence and returned to London, where he held several administrative posts before retiring to Marrakesh in 1968. He died in 1981.

Known as 'The Auk' to his troops, General Auchinleck was C-in-C Middle East from July 1941 to August 1942. (IWM)

11

Marshal Pietro Badoglio
Italian Army

Pietro Badoglio was born on 28 September 1871, in Monferrato, Italy. He entered the Italian Army in 1890 as an artillery officer and fought with distinction in Ethiopia in 1896 and in the Italo-Turkish War of 1912. During World War I, he distinguished himself by directing the capture of Monte Sabotino on 6 August 1916. This occurred during a major Italian offensive on the Isonzo, and was one of the Italian Army's more notable actions of the war; after a tremendous bombardment, the Italians took Sabotino ridge, Hill 188, Podgora ridge and town, Monte Calvario, Monte San Michele ridge and Hill 85, east of Monfalcone. It was a very different story at Caporetto on 24 October 1917, when the Austrians and Germans counter-attacked on the Isonzo Front and inflicted a resounding defeat on the Second Italian Army, taking thousands of prisoners.

Despite being held partly responsible for failing to prevent this enemy success, Badoglio emerged from the war with his career intact, participated in the Armistice talks for the Italians and was Chief of Staff from 1919 to 1921. Badoglio was at first only lukewarm towards Mussolini and stayed out of politics for a year before serving as Ambassador to Brazil. In 1925 Mussolini named him Chief of Staff, and he was promoted field marshal on 26 May 1926. He was Governor of Libya from 1928 to 1934, and in 1936 he commanded the forces that captured Addis Ababa, the capital of Ethiopia, where he was subsequently installed as Viceroy.

Badoglio resigned as Chief of Staff during the Italian Army's disastrous campaign in Greece, where the small and poorly equipped Greek army inflicted one defeat after another on the numerically superior Italians, and disclaimed responsibility for Mussolini's actions. He remained in the background until the downfall of Mussolini on 25 July 1943, which he helped to engineer. Badoglio then became Prime Minister of Italy and quickly arranged for an armistice with the Allies on 3 September, which was followed by the unconditional surrender of Italy on 8 September. Badoglio dissolved the Fascist Party and declared war on Germany on 13 October 1943. In June 1944 he resigned to allow the formation of a new government in liberated Rome, and retired to his family home, where he died on 1 November 1956.

Marshal Pietro Badoglio (right) pictured with Werner von Blomberg, the German Minister of War from 1935 to 1938. The meeting may have been in connection with the participation of Germany and Italy in the Spanish Civil War. (Bundesarchiv)

Generalfeldmarschall Fedor von Bock
German Army

A highly experienced and much decorated soldier, Fedor von Bock was placed at the head of the armies that conducted Germany's Blitzkrieg campaigns at the outset of World War II. (Bundesarchiv)

Fedor von Bock was born in Küstrin (Kostrzyn), Poland, on 3 December 1880, the son of an army officer. In 1898 he was commissioned into the 5th Guards Infantry Regiment, and by 1907 he had reached the position of battalion adjutant. During World War I, as a general staff officer and battalion commander, Bock served on both the Eastern and Western Fronts, and in 1918, in recognition of his achievements in the Picardy (Ludendorff) offensive, he received the Ordre Pour le Mérite, Germany's highest decoration. Remaining in the army after the war, he was promoted general in the army of the Weimar Republic in 1919. A succession of appointments followed, and although he was not an overt supporter of the Nazis he soon rose to high rank in the Wehrmacht. In March 1938 he marched into Austria at the head of the German Eighth Army, and later in the year he was appointed commander of Army Group One.

In September/October 1938 Bock commanded Army Group North during the campaign in Poland, and during the assault on the West in May/June 1940 he commanded Army Group B, which advanced with lightning speed through the Low Countries. In July 1941, as a Generalfeldmarschall, he was appointed commander of the German forces of occupation in western Poland. In the following year he commanded Army Group Centre in the invasion of Russia, and was blamed by Hitler for the German failure to capture Moscow. His cause was not helped by his pleas for a tactical withdrawal, and he was relieved of his command, but in January 1942 he was given command of Army Group South following the sudden death of its previous commander. In the months that followed he was criticized for dividing the army group between Stalingrad and the Caucasus, and in July he was again relieved of his command and sent into retirement.

He languished until May 1945, when, following Hitler's suicide, he was invited to become part of the new German leadership at Flensburg. On 3 May, he was severely injured in a low-level attack by RAF aircraft, and died in hospital the next day.

General Omar Bradley
US Army

In the 12th Army Group, General Omar Bradley commanded one of the largest and tactically most important formations ever to take the field in war. (US Army)

Omar Nelson Bradley was born in Clark, Missouri, on 12 February 1893. He graduated from the US Military Academy at West Point in 1915 and subsequently reached the temporary rank of major while serving with the 14th Infantry Regiment. Early in World War II he served as commandant of the Infantry School, commanded an infantry division in training, and in the spring of 1943 commanded the US II Corps in North Africa, later moving with it to Sicily. He was selected by the Supreme Allied Commander, General Dwight Eisenhower, to command the US First Army, which was to spearhead the American contribution to the invasion of Normandy in June 1944. With the Allies safely ashore and a breakout from the Normandy beach-head imminent, Bradley was appointed to command the US 12th Army Group, which by the spring of 1945 would comprise four field armies – twelve corps, 48 divisions and more than 1,300,000 men.

Following the breakout from Normandy, Bradley's forces pushed on to liberate Paris and advanced towards the Rhine. In the winter of 1944–5 they bore the brunt of the German counter-offensive in the Ardennes, and in March 1945 they established a bridgehead over the Rhine at Remagen, subsequently advancing on a broad front to effect a link-up with Soviet forces at the Elbe. In 1948 Bradley was appointed Chief of Staff of the US Army, and in 1949 he became Chairman of the Joint Chiefs of Staff, a position he held until 1953. In September 1950, while in this post, the became the fourth US officer to reach the five-star rank of general of the army. He also served as the first chairman of the Military Committee of the North Atlantic Treaty Organization. After relinquishing the NATO Military Committee chairmanship in 1950, Bradley continued to serve until 1953 as US representative on the committee and on its Standing Group.

General Eisenhower, who had a high opinion of Bradley, dating back to their days together at West Point, spoke of 'his ability and reputation as a sound, painstaking, and broadly educated soldier'. In fact, with his mild manner and high-pitched voice, the image he put over was less that of a soldier than of a schoolteacher, which he actually was during much of his early army career.

General Omar Bradley died in New York City on 8 April 1981.

General Omar Bradley conferring with a Soviet general after the meeting of US and Russian forces on the Elbe. (US Army)

Generalfeldmarschall Walther von Brauchitsch
German Army

Born in Berlin on 4 October 1881, Walther von Brauchitsch was the son of General Bernhard von Brauchitsch and his wife Charlotte. Following the inevitable path of a Prussian officer's son, Walther completed his training at officer cadet school and was commissioned into the 3rd Queen Elizabeth Guards Grenadier Regiment in 1900. During World War I he served as a staff officer in various units, and in 1921 he became a major in the Reichswehr, being responsible mainly for training. In 1927 he was appointed Chief of Staff of Defence Sector (Wehrkreis) VI, and in the following year he was promoted to Oberst. In 1929 he was placed in charge of Reichswehr training at the Defence Ministry, and in 1931 he was dispatched to Russia to set up a Reichswehr training scheme with the co-operation of the Red Army. In 1936 he was appointed commander of Wehrkreis I in East Prussia.

In 1938 von Brauchitsch was appointed Army Supreme Commander (Oberbefehlshaber des Heers), in which capacity he conducted the campaigns in Poland, France and Russia during World War II. He was often in conflict with Hitler over the latter's political and military decisions, but could make no headway; his requests to be allowed to resign were repeatedly turned down, and in 1940 he was made a Generalfeldmarschall. In December 1941, however, Hitler held von Brauchitsch personally responsible for the failure of the German offensive in Russia, and personally replaced him as commander-in-chief. He lapsed into relative obscurity until July 1944, when he publicly condemned the attempt on Hitler's life; but he also spoke on behalf of some of the accused. In 1945–6 he was called as a witness at the Allied war crimes tribunal. He was himself arraigned on lesser charges, but on 18 October 1948, before he could stand trial, he died in British military custody, having suffered a succession of heart attacks.

Adolf Hitler held Generalfeldmarschall von Brauchitsch personally responsible for the failure of the 1941 offensive in Russia, and replaced him. (Bundesarchiv)

Marshal Semyon Budenny
Soviet Army

Like many of his contemporaries, Semyon Budenny, who was born on 13 April 1883 at Rostov-on-Don in the heart of Cossack country, served as an NCO in the Imperial Russian Army, only rising to prominence after he joined the Red Army in the aftermath of the Revolution. He proved himself to be an able leader during the Russo-Polish war of 1920 when, commanding the 1st Cavalry Army, he attacked the southern Polish flank and broke through to capture Kiev. Three months later, however, the Russians were decisively beaten at the gates of Warsaw.

Budenny, who set great store by his personal image, sporting a huge moustache and personalized revolvers, survived the purges of the 1930s, being made a Marshal of the Soviet Union in 1935, and was one of the senior Soviet commanders in Russia's disastrous and costly 'Winter War' of 1939–40 against Finland. By the summer of 1941, when the Germans launched their invasion of Russia, he was vice-commissar of defence and in command of the Soviet group of armies on the south-western front, covering the Ukraine and Bessarabia. At Kiev, which Stalin wanted held at all costs, Budenny failed hopelessly to defend the city against a much smaller German force, lost over a million men, and then – obeying Stalin's scorched earth policy to the letter – destroyed both Kiev and a great dam spanning the River Dnieper, bringing industry in the eastern Ukraine to a virtual standstill. Nevertheless, although Budenny's armies were dispersed, they were not trapped, as the Germans hoped they would be. The hard core of the Soviet forces drew away, just out of reach of German encircling movements, as they would do time and again.

Budenny was relieved of his command, but was later placed in charge of the Soviet army group on the northern Caucasus front, although much of his time was spent in training recruits. Despite his failings, he was made Inspector of Cavalry in 1953. He died in 1973, in his ninetieth year.

Dashing and flamboyant, Budenny proved utterly incompetent as an army commander. (via J. R. Cavanagh)

Admiral Wilhelm Canaris
German Navy

Although Admiral Canaris wanted to see Adolf Hitler toppled from power, he had no wish to see him assassinated. (Bundesarchiv)

Wilhelm Canaris, a man who might have had a decisive impact on history, was born on 1 January 1887 in Aplerbeck, Westphalia, the son of an industrialist. In 1905 he was commissioned into the Imperial German Navy, and in 1914 he took part in the Falklands Battle as an officer on board the heavy cruiser *Dresden*. When the latter was sunk by Royal Navy warships off Juan Fernandez in March 1915, Canaris was interned in Chile, but by various means made his way back to Germany. In 1916, as a Kapitänleutnant, he undertook a special mission to Spain on behalf of the German Admiralty, and in the last two years of the war he commanded a U-boat in the Mediterranean.

In 1920 Canaris was appointed to the Admiral's Staff of the Baltic Fleet, and held a number of staff and seagoing commands until 1933, when he enthusiastically accepted the rise of the Nazi Party. In 1935 he was appointed head of the Admiralty Intelligence Section as a Konteradmiral; this soon expanded into the Abwehr, embracing all the German armed forces. In 1939, he repeatedly and vainly warned influential Nazis of the danger of launching a war, and even sought to persuade Benito Mussolini against it. In 1940 Canaris reached the rank of Admiral. His real opposition to the Nazi Party developed after the attack on the Soviet Union in 1941, when he learned of the German Army's excesses in Russia. His growing disillusionment with the Nazis became known to their leadership, and in 1943 he was placed under constant observation.

In 1944, the defection of an Abwehr agent to the British gave the Nazis an excuse to dismiss Canaris from his post. Three days after the attempt on Hitler's life (the 'bomb plot' of July 1944) Canaris was arrested and implicated. Even though he had always opposed any attempt to kill Hitler, he had lent his active support to factions seeking to overthrow him, and the damning evidence that emerged during his trial was enough to put him in a concentration camp. He was executed in April 1945, as American forces approached the camp at Flossenburg.

17

Neville Chamberlain
British Prime Minister

The British Prime Minister, Neville Chamberlain, making his famous 'peace in our time' speech after the 1938 Munich conference. (author's collection)

The son of Joseph Chamberlain and half-brother of Sir Austen, Arthur Neville Chamberlain was born in Birmingham in 1869 and educated there. In 1915, after a successful career in business, he became chairman of Birmingham City Council. Elected to Parliament in 1918, he served as Postmaster-General in 1922–3 and had three terms as Minister of Health, in 1923, 1924–9 and 1931. He was twice Chancellor of the Exchequer, in 1923–4 and 1931–7, before succeeding Stanley Baldwin as Prime Minister. During his second term as Chancellor of the Exchequer he drastically curtailed expenditure on armaments, only reversing the process with various armed forces' expansion schemes in the late 1930s when the extent of German rearmament became apparent. His principal aim as Prime Minister was to avoid another European war at all costs – a policy that led him along the path of appeasement. Too late, following the Munich crisis of 1938, he recognized the failure of this policy, and after the Germans marched into the Czech Sudetenland in March 1939 he vowed to support Poland if that country should be attacked by Germany.

Poland was attacked, precipitating World War II, and it was now that the folly of Britain's headlong rush towards disarmament in the inter-war years became clear. One disaster followed another, beginning with the disastrous campaign in Norway in April 1940 and culminating in the German assault on France and the Low Countries in May 1940, resulting in the evacuation of the British Expeditionary Force. By then, Chamberlain's political career was already doomed. Following the débâcle in Norway his parliamentary majority fell from 250 votes to 81 in a crucial debate on 7/8 May. He resigned two days later and was succeeded as Prime Minister by Winston Churchill.

Chamberlain served in Churchill's cabinet as Lord President of the Council until October 1940, when illness compelled him to resign. He died in the following month. Despite his failings and misconceptions, history should not treat Neville Chamberlain too harshly. His decision to appease the dictators Hitler and Mussolini was a reflection of his cabinet's and the nation's wishes, and the achievement of 'peace in our time' pursuant to the signing of the Munich Pact was briefly held to be a diplomatic success. His highly publicized flying visits to various summit conferences in an attempt to preserve European peace were an early example of shuttle diplomacy.

Major-General Claire Lee Chennault
US Army Air Force

Born on 6 September 1893 in Commerce, Texas, Claire Chennault was descended from eighteenth-century Huguenot immigrants. He was raised and educated in Louisiana, and attended Louisiana State University. Afterwards, he was a school teacher in Louisiana, Mississippi and Kentucky before training as a flying instructor upon America's entry into World War I. Commissioned as a 1st lieutenant, he flew with the US Border Patrol from 1919 to 1923 and with the Hawaiian Pursuit Squadron until 1926. He subsequently served with the US Pursuit Development Board and the Air Corps Exhibition Group in the 1930s. In 1937, partly because of problems with his hearing and partly because of ongoing disagreements with his superiors, he was forced into retirement.

Later that year, he went to China at the request of Chiang Kai-shek's government to carry out a survey of the Chinese Air Force, which was in a woeful state. Its shortcomings became apparent in July 1937, when the Japanese invaded Manchuria and began pushing inland. For the next three years Chennault, who rose to the rank of colonel in the Chinese Air Force, did his utmost to resolve its

problems, but it was not until October 1940 that he was authorized to purchase modern fighter aircraft from the USA and recruit experienced pilots to fly them. The result was the famous Flying Tigers, an international air squadron formed under the cover of an organization called the Central Aircraft Manufacturing Company (CAMCO), equipped with Curtiss P-40B fighters and manned by volunteers who were all serving US military personnel.

The achievement of the Flying Tigers in action against the Japanese Air Force became legendary. In a six-month period during 1941–2 they destroyed some 300 Japanese aircraft, and Chennault's success contributed to his return to the US military as a major-general, commanding the Fourteenth Air Force in the China–Burma–India theatre. Disagreements with his new superior officer and theatre commander, General Joseph Stilwell, led to a second enforced retirement in July 1945. Afterwards, he founded a company called Civil Air Transport, which became a covert arm of the Central Intelligence Agency.

Claire Chennault died of cancer on 27 July 1958.

Claire Chennault's American Volunteer Group showed what determined pilots could do to the Japanese, provided the tactics were sound and the equipment modern. (USAF)

Generalissimo Chiang Kai-Shek
Chinese Nationalist Statesman

Generalissimo Chiang Kai-shek had to contend not only with the invading Japanese, but with the Communists in his own backyard.
(Encarta Online)

Born in 1887, the man who was destined to become the Chinese Nationalist leader studied military affairs in Japan and later served briefly in the Japanese Army. Returning to China in 1911, he became involved in the revolt against the Manchu dynasty. Chiang remained politically active from this time, and in 1926, when he emerged as successor to Sun Yat-sen as leader of the Nationalist Party, he led the victorious Nationalist (Kuomintang) Army, initially co-operating with Communist factions and accepting aid from the Soviet Union in an attempt to unify China. In 1927, however, he changed his policy and initiated a war against the Communists that was to last for more than two decades.

By the end of 1927 Chiang had become head of the Nationalist government, and as such was supreme commander of all Nationalist forces. In 1937, on the outbreak of the Sino-Japanese war, he elected to use his best troops in the ongoing fight against the Communists, recognizing that Mao Zedong's hard-bitten guerrilla forces would use the situation to gain ground. During World War II Chiang became supreme commander of all Allied forces in the China theatre, and in the lengthy struggle against the Japanese he earned great prestige among the Allied leadership, even though he was often at odds with it. By the time he attended the Cairo Conference of Allied leaders in 1943, he was undisputed master of China, but after the expulsion of the Japanese in 1945 civil war once again erupted between the Communists and the Kuomintang. In 1947 the Communist forces mounted a general offensive, gaining a series of victories, and when the commander of the Beijing-Tainjin region surrendered to the Communists early in 1949, the Nationalist cause collapsed. In 1950, Chiang and the Nationalists evacuated to Formosa (Taiwan), from which base he promised to reconquer the Chinese mainland, but the recognition by the United Nations of the Communists as sole rulers of China in 1972 dashed any such hope.

Chiang Kai-shek died in 1975.

General Vassili Chuikov
Soviet Army

Born in 1900, Vassili Chuikov joined the Red Army in 1919 and was quickly promoted, mainly because of his membership of the Communist Party. Tough and with unbreakable nerve, he possessed great tactical ability, but was a loyal subordinate rather than an initiator of strategy. He graduated from the Frunze Military Academy in the 1920s and was adviser to the Chinese Nationalist Leader Chiang Kai-shek from 1926 to 1937. He made a thorough study of mechanized warfare, and commanded the Soviet 9th Army in the 'Winter War' between Finland and the Soviet Union in 1939–40, a conflict that saw ill-led Soviet forces decisively beaten by a far smaller but much more effective Finnish Army. He returned to China, but was hastily recalled when the Germans launched Operation Barbarossa in June 1941. In March 1942 he took command of the 64th Army, and later in the year was made commander of the 62nd Army in Stalingrad, using all his reserves of manpower to defend the city against the German onslaught, his tactics being to place units in isolated parts of the city to build pockets of resistance, which led the Germans to over-estimate the number of Soviet troops actually involved in the defence. Although the Russians lost ground, the German Sixth Army lost enormous quantities of men and material in their efforts to eliminate these pockets of resistance, as well as using up vital reserves of fuel, which could not be replaced by air once Stalingrad had been surrounded by the Red Army's counter-offensives.

After Stalingrad, Chuikov commanded various formations, notably the 8th Guards Army, which was sent to the Byelorussian Front to spearhead the drive into Germany, beginning with the liberation of Poland – an offensive that was temporarily halted at the Vistula on the orders of Stalin in August 1944 while the Germans crushed the Polish Home Army in Warsaw. Fittingly, it was Chuikov who received the surrender of Berlin from General Krebs in May 1945. Post war, Chuikov commanded the Soviet army of occupation in Germany from 1945 to 1953 – a time of great tension that saw the blockade of Berlin. General Chuikov died in 1982.

Soviet troops fighting in the ruins of Stalingrad, a city desperately defended by Chuikov. (via J. R. Cavanagh)

Sir Winston Leonard Spencer Churchill
British Prime Minister

The most famous British national leader of all time, Winston Churchill found his fame in directing the nation through the dark days of World War II. (IWM)

Born in 1874, Winston Churchill was the son of Lord Randolph Churchill. He was educated at Harrow, entered the Royal Military Academy, Sandhurst, and in 1894 was commissioned into the 4th Hussars. In 1895, while on leave, he witnessed military action for the first time, when he was in Cuba, acting as a reporter for the *London Daily Graphic*. As a subaltern, he subsequently saw active service in India and the Sudan, where he took part in the last great British cavalry charge at Omdurman in 1898. He subsequently resigned his commission and travelled to South Africa, where he covered the Boer War as a war correspondent with the *Morning Post*. He was captured by the Boers in 1899 but escaped, a feat that made him a household name in Britain.

In 1900 Churchill was elected to Parliament as a Conservative; later, he crossed the floor of the House and became a Liberal. He climbed the political ladder rapidly, serving first as Under-Secretary for the Colonies, then (1908–10) as President of the Board of Trade and as Home Secretary in 1910–11. In the latter year he became First Lord of the Admiralty and oversaw the final stages of the modernization of the British Fleet, a process begun a decade earlier. In July 1914 Churchill, convinced that war with Germany was imminent, ordered the main body of the fleet, which had just been reviewed by King George V at Spithead, to sail to Scapa Flow in the Orkneys instead of dispersing to naval bases all around the British Isles. There, it posed a constant threat to the German High Seas Fleet, which apart from venturing out to fight the Battle of Jutland in May 1916, remained penned up in its north German harbours until the end of the war.

Churchill was the champion of the Allied expedition to the Dardanelles, an imaginative operation that failed because of inadequate planning and a lack of initiative on the part of its commanders. It resulted in the loss of Churchill's post at the Admiralty, and in 1916 he returned to the army, commanding an infantry battalion on the Western Front as a major. He re-entered politics after David Lloyd George became Prime Minister, and was successively Minister of Munitions (1917–19), War Secretary (1919–21) and Colonial Secretary (1921–2). From 1924 to 1929, a Conservative once more, he served as Chancellor of the Exchequer; then the Conservatives were defeated at the polls, and he was suddenly out of office.

In the decade that followed, during which he campaigned ceaselessly for British rearmament and warned constantly of the rise of fascism, he wrote some of his greatest works. In 1939, at the outbreak of war, he was appointed to his former post as First Lord of the Admiralty by Neville Chamberlain; and on 10 May 1940, when the Germans launched their invasion of western Europe and Chamberlain resigned, it was Churchill who replaced him as Prime Minister.

Churchill's stirring power of oratory, his boundless energy and his steadfast refusal to conclude a peace with the Nazis played an incalculable part in cementing the resolve of the British people during the grim years of 1940–41. Afterwards, he made major contributions to Allied strategy, particularly in persuading the Americans that the defeat of Germany should be their first objective – a wise move, given the fact that German scientists were pursuing atomic weapons research. Throughout the war, Churchill possessed immense power, but in July 1945 he and the Conservatives were defeated in the General Election by Clement Attlee's Labour Party. He was returned as Prime Minister in 1951 and again in 1955, but resigned shortly afterwards in favour of Anthony Eden. In 1953 he was appointed a Knight of the Garter and was awarded the Nobel Prize for Literature. He died in January 1965, having suffered a massive stroke, and was accorded a state funeral. He was 90 years old.

General Mark Wayne Clark
US Army

Mark Clark was born in Madison Barrack, New York, in 1896. He graduated from the United States Military Academy at West Point in 1917 and served in France during the last year of World War I. After continuous service in the US Army, he arrived in England in 1942 to take command of the US Second Army. He came to prominence in November 1942, during Operation Torch, the invasion of North Africa, which had been forced on the reluctant Combined Chiefs of Staff by Roosevelt and Churchill. The US Chiefs of Staff never lost their dislike of the operation, which they regarded, rightly, as likely to delay the invasion of north-west Europe until 1944; the British Chiefs of Staff, however, soon became enthusiastic supporters. The American Lieutenant-General Dwight D. Eisenhower was placed in supreme command, with a British naval commander, Admiral Sir Andrew Cunningham, under him; while the commanders of the land forces for all three initial landings were to be American generals until their forces, once ashore, combined to form the First Army under Lieutenant-General Sir Kenneth Anderson, with Major-General Mark Clark as his deputy.

Prior to the landings, Clark made a secret and very hazardous trip in HM Submarine *Seraph* to reconnoitre the Algerian coastline, and after the landings it was Clark, acting as Eisenhower's personal emissary, who negotiated with the anti-British Admiral Darlan for the surrender of Vichy French forces in the area. Later in the year, Clark was promoted to lieutenant-general and given command of the Fifth Army, which landed in Italy in September. At Salerno, Clark personally took command of Allied units and directed the destruction of a German counter-attack. On 1 October Clark's forces captured Naples, but were unable to break through the strongly fortified Gustav Line, and in an attempt to outflank the enemy he organized an amphibious landing at Anzio in January 1944. This nearly ended in catastrophe when the Allies lost the element of surprise and encountered unexpectedly strong enemy resistance, the situation only being saved by heavy naval gunfire support. On the other hand, Clark's troops entered Rome on 5 June 1944, an achievement that was eclipsed when the news broke the next day that the Allies were ashore in Normandy.

Clark was now in command of the 15th Army Group, which comprised all Allied forces operating in Italy. At the war's end in 1945 he was placed in command of the Allied forces of occupation in Austria and appointed US High Commissioner there, playing a key part in negotiating the country's future in the post-war world. In 1952, General Clark replaced General Matthew Ridgway as commander of the UN forces in Korea, and it was he who signed an armistice with the Chinese People's Republic and North Korea at Panmunjom on 27 July 1953.

General Mark Clark died in 1984 and is buried at the Citadel campus, Charleston, South Carolina, adjacent to Mark Clark Hall.

General Mark Clark conducted a particularly difficult and dangerous war in Italy, where his campaigns were overshadowed by those in north-west Europe. (US Army)

General Lucius D. Clay
US Army

General Lucius Clay (right), conferring with General Sir Brian Robertson and General Pierre Koenig, commanders of the British and French Zones of Berlin, at the time of the Airlift. (AP)

Lucius DuBignon Clay was born in Marietta, Georgia, on 23 April 1897, the son of a US Senator. He entered the US Military Academy, West Point, in 1915 and graduated as an army engineer in 1918, returning to the Academy in 1924 to teach military and civil engineering for a four-year period. After a number of engineering assignments he joined the staff of General MacArthur in 1937, and in 1940–41 headed a programme that involved the upgrading of 277 civil airports in the US so that they would be suitable for military use, and supervising the building of 197 new ones.

By 1942 Clay had risen to the rank of brigadier-general, the youngest in the US Army. He was appointed Assistant Chief of Staff for Materiel (Service of Supply), and when the latter was reorganized he became Director of Materiel, Army Service Forces. In June 1944, shortly after D-Day, Clay masterminded an operation that proved vital to the Allied breakout from Normandy and subsequent drive into France – the clearance of the port of Cherbourg, vital for the flow of supplies. The port had been seriously damaged by the Germans, and the harbour basins were thickly sown with contact mines, most of which were cleared by British divers, working day and night. By the middle of July the port had been sufficiently cleared to allow a limited flow of traffic, but it was not restored to its full potential until the middle of August. Nevertheless, it was a remarkable achievement which earned Clay a Bronze Star.

In March 1947 Clay succeeded General Eisenhower as Military Governor of Germany, and it was in that capacity that he masterminded the Berlin Airlift of 1948–9, implemented when the Russians imposed a blockade of the city. This is the achievement for which Clay is best remembered, his vital engineering work in World War II having largely been overshadowed by the activities of the field commanders.

General Lucius Clay retired in May, 1949, a few weeks after the blockade was lifted. He died on 16 April 1978.

General Joseph L. Collins
US Army

Joseph Lawton Collins was born in 1896, the son of Irish immigrant parents. He attended the US Military Academy, West Point, and graduated in 1917, being commissioned into the infantry. His progress up the promotion ladder was steady, and on the outbreak of World War II he was appointed Chief of Staff of the newly formed US VI Corps in Birmingham, Alabama. After the Japanese attack on Pearl Harbor in December 1941, he became Chief of Staff in the Hawaiian Department, with the task of organizing the area's defences; it was the beginning of a pacific tour that was to last three years.

In 1942 Collins was promoted brigadier-general, and later in the year he was given command of the 25th Infantry, which relieved the US Marines on the island of Guadalcanal. In January 1943 Collins led his troops in some of the most savage fighting seen so far, as the Japanese fought to retain a toe-hold on the island at Kokumbona, but they were forced to evacuate early in February.

Collins's achievements in the final stages of the Guadalcanal campaign placed him in line for promotion to three-star general, but the Allied commander, General Douglas MacArthur, opposed this on the grounds that Collins was too young. The US Army Chief of Staff, General George C. Marshall, recognized Collins's potential and had him transferred to the European theatre, and in February 1944 he was given command of the US VII Corps, which was training in England in preparation for the Allied landings in Normandy. After D-Day, it was VII Corps, under Collins's dynamic leadership, that fought its way across the base of the Cotentin Peninsula to capture the port of Cherbourg on 27 June. Collins's Corps then led the breakout from the Normandy bridgehead at St-Lô on 25 July.

Later, soldiers of VII Corps were the first to reach German soil, capturing Aachen. They subsequently took Cologne on 11 March 1945, and after the surrender of German forces in the Remagen area they raced on to the Elbe, which was reached on 25 April, an event that coincided with Collins's promotion to lieutenant-general. He remained in Europe after the war, and in 1947 he was appointed deputy chief of staff to General Eisenhower. Promoted full general in 1948, he became US Army Chief of Staff, and was instrumental in the formation of NATO.

General Joseph 'Lightning Joe' Collins retired in 1956 and died in Washington on 12 September 1987.

General Joseph L. Collins

Air Marshal Sir Arthur Coningham
Royal Air Force

Arthur Coningham pictured in 1944, when he was AOC-in-C the RAF 2nd Tactical Air Force. (RAF)

Known in his early years by the nickname 'Maori', soon corrupted to 'Mary' by his colleagues in the Royal Flying Corps, Arthur Coningham was born in Brisbane, Australia, in 1895 and was educated at Wellington College, New Zealand. He joined the New Zealand Army on the outbreak of World War I and saw service in the Middle East before transferring to the Royal Flying Corps in 1916. He subsequently served with Nos 32 and 92 Squadrons, ending the war as a major, DSO, MC, with fourteen victories to his credit. Remaining in the post-war RAF, in October 1925, while commanding No. 47 Squadron in the Middle East, he led three DH 9A aircraft on a record-breaking pioneering flight from Helwan, Egypt, to Kano, Nigeria, opening up a route that would be used for the air reinforcement of the North African theatre in WWII.

In July 1939 Coningham, now an air vice-marshal, was given command of No. 4 Group, RAF Bomber Command, which comprised eight squadrons equipped with Armstrong Whitworth Whitleys. In July 1941 he was posted back to the Middle East to command No. 204 Group, and in December he became Air Officer Commanding, Western Desert. In this capacity he pioneered the use of tactical air power, and also introduced the idea of small bomber formations protected by large numbers of fighters.

Coningham received a knighthood after the Battle of El Alamein in 1942, and his Desert Air Force continued to support General Montgomery's Eighth Army as it drove towards Tunisia to link up with the Allied forces that landed in North Africa in November. In the Tunisian campaign, as an air marshal, he commanded the North-West African Tactical Air Force, and in the summer of 1943 he directed tactical air operations during the invasions of Sicily and Italy. At the end of 1943, Coningham went to England to become a key member of the team that was planning the forthcoming Allied landings in Normandy, for which he was appointed Air Officer Commanding-in-Chief, RAF 2nd Tactical Air Force. He remained in command of 2nd TAF until the end of the war, setting up his HQ in Brussels. His last major task was to plan the air support for the crossing of the Rhine, which took place in March 1945.

An extremely able commander, Air Marshal Coningham was responsible for many important developments in Allied tactical air power, particularly in the theory and practice of close air support. He lost his life on 30 January 1948, when the Avro Tudor of British South African Airways in which he was flying as a passenger went missing over the Atlantic.

General Henry Crerar
Canadian Army

Born in Hamilton, Ontario, in 1888, Henry Crerar trained at the Royal Military College and went on to have a distinguished career in World War I. Between the wars, he became Director of Military Operations and Intelligence, and also served as Commandant of the Royal Military College. In 1939 he requested an overseas posting, and as a brigadier he was attached to the Canadian Military HQ in London in 1940. Made Chief of the Canadian General Staff in 1941, Crerar was responsible for the dispatch of Canadian troops to Hong Kong shortly before the Japanese attack, after which most went into captivity. In 1942, he assumed command of the Canadian Corps in Britain, and led it in the absence of its usual commander, General MacNaughton, during the disastrous raid at Dieppe in August that year. He also had the difficult task of expanding the Canadian Army at a time when there was much dispute over conscription. Wishing to see active service, he secured command of the 1st Canadian Corps, which he led in Sicily in the summer of 1943. At the end of the year, when General MacNaughton was recalled to Canada, he was given command of the 1st Canadian Army, which was preparing for the invasion of Europe.

During the Normandy campaign he came under the orders of Field Marshal Montgomery, who clashed with him over who should command the Canadian forces and attempted to restrict his area of responsibility. When Crerar was forced to return to England through illness, his command was taken over by General Simonds, who was given the task of capturing the Scheldt Estuary. When Crerar returned to active duty, he proceeded to confound his critics by conducting a series of brilliant military actions, which culminated in the breaking of the Siegfried Line on 27 February 1945. By this time, the forces under his command comprised Canadians, Americans, Poles and British.

General Henry Crerar died in 1965.

General Crerar (left), pictured in Normandy with the Supreme Allied Commander, General Dwight D. Eisenhower. (National Archives)

Generalleutnant Ludwig Crüwell
German Army

Crüwell might have had a spectacular career with the Afrika Korps had he not been captured by the British after his aircraft was forced down. (Bundesarchiv)

A skilful and level-headed general, Ludwig Crüwell might have had a decisive impact on the conduct of the German Afrika Korps had he not been captured by the British at a crucial juncture, as Rommel was planning his final offensive into Egypt. Born in Dortmund on 20 March 1892, Crüwell was a career soldier who was twice awarded the Iron Cross (2nd and 1st Class respectively) in 1914 and 1916; he was to receive Bars to both these decorations in 1939. He remained in the German Army after World War I, reaching the rank of Oberstleutnant in April 1934. In March 1936 he was promoted to Oberst, and June 1944 December 1939, as a Generalmajor, he assumed command of 5 Panzer Division, which he led during the campaign in France. In May 1940 he was awarded the Knight's Cross in recognition of his services. Further appointments, and promotion, followed swiftly; on 1 August 1940 he was given command of 11 Panzer Division, one of the formations poised for the invasion of England; but the invasion never took place, and instead the division was diverted to the campaigns in the Balkans in April 1941, and in Russia two months later. In September 1941 Crüwell was promoted to Generalleutnant, at the same time receiving the Oak Leaves to his Knight's Cross, and in December he was appointed General der Panzertruppen, a post that made him responsible for all the Wehrmacht's armoured formations.

Crüwell was appointed to command the Deutsches Afrika Korps (DAK) at the end of 1941. It was an ideal appointment, for by now he had much experience of mobile armoured warfare. His handling of the DAK during Rommel's counter-attack following the British offensive of 1941–2 (Operation Crusader) was nothing short of masterly, and it was perhaps fortunate for the British that he was out of action with jaundice in March and April. He was back in the line in May 1942, when Rommel attacked towards Gazala, and it was thanks in the main to his planning that the DAK was able to punch its way around the southern end of the heavily mined Gazala Line and, after withstanding heavy attacks, to break out eastwards in the armoured dash that would be halted at Alamein. Crüwell, however, was destined to see none of this: on 29 May 1942, the Fieseler Storch liaison aircraft in which he was flying was forced down and he was captured by the British. Released from captivity in 1947, he died on 25 September 1958 in Essen.

Admiral of the Fleet Viscount Cunningham
Royal Navy

Like many other men who were to rise to senior rank in the British armed forces, Andrew Browne Cunningham was an Irishman by birth, born in Dublin on 7 January 1883. In fact, his father was a Scot, an Edinburgh professor. Cunningham joined the Royal Navy in 1897 as a cadet and served with the Naval Brigade in the South African War. From 1911 to 1918 he commanded the destroyer HMS *Scorpion*, serving with distinction in the Gallipoli campaign and on the Dover patrol. Between 1918 and 1938 he commanded the battleship HMS *Rodney*, the Mediterranean destroyer flotillas and finally, as a vice-admiral, the Mediterranean battlecruiser squadron. In November 1938 he became Deputy Chief of Naval Staff, but in the following year he was re-appointed to the Mediterranean as Commander-in-Chief, in preparation for the growing likelihood of war with Germany and her Axis partner, Italy.

As Commander-in-Chief, Admiral Cunningham ordered the Fleet Air Arm attack on Taranto in November 1940, a masterly stroke which crippled half the Italian Battle Fleet and which convincingly demonstrated the effectiveness of carrier-based air power. The lesson was not lost on the Japanese, who put the principles into practice even more convincingly at Pearl Harbor, just over a year later. In April 1941, after the Battle of Cape Matapan, Admiral Cunningham organized the evacuation of the British Army from Greece and Crete. Both operations were successful, though lack of air support resulted in very severe naval losses.

Admiral Cunningham left the Mediterranean in the spring of 1942, embarking on a tour of the United States before assuming the post of Naval Commander-in-Chief for the Allied invasion of North Africa (Operation Torch). In February 1943 he returned as C-in-C Mediterranean, and in July supervised the Allied landings on Sicily. In September, he had the satisfaction of receiving the surrender of the Italian fleet at Malta before returning to Britain as First Sea Lord, a post he held until the end of the war. In June 1945 he retired, after almost half a century in the Royal Navy, and was created Viscount Hyndhope. Admiral of the Fleet Viscount Cunningham of Hyndhope KG, GCB, OM, DSO died in London on 12 June 1963.

Admiral Cunningham, seen here on the left, conducted difficult and dangerous naval operations in the Mediterranean in 1940–42. (IWM)

Admiral Jean François Darlan
French Navy

In June 1940, after Dunkirk, with the collapse of France imminent, there was one important goal which the British failed to achieve, and that was to persuade the French government to allow its powerful fleet to sail to British ports and carry on the struggle alongside the Royal Navy. Although most of its capital ships escaped capture by the Germans, they sailed for ports in the French colonies, principally North Africa.

The man who ordered this action was Admiral Jean François Darlan, an officer whose intense dislike of the British was well known. Born on 7 August 1881 at Nerac, Lot-et-Garonne, Darlan graduated from the Ecole Navale in 1901 and served with distinction in World War I. In 1925 he was appointed liaison officer to the Navy Minister, returning to active duty in 1934 as commander of the French Atlantic Fleet. In 1936 he was made Chief of Staff of the French Navy, and could claim with justification that by 1940 he had turned the French fleet into a viable force, equipped with modern warships of excellent design.

His dislike of the British turned to open hatred when, in July 1940, Winston Churchill ordered the Royal Navy to destroy the French fleet in order to prevent its seizure by the Axis. At this time Darlan was Navy Minister in the Vichy French government under Marshal Pétain, and he went out of his way to provide the Germans with information about the vital British base of Gibraltar, partly to ingratiate himself and partly out of revenge. In December 1940 he was elevated to the position of deputy premier, and two months later he was nominated as Pétain's successor. In 1941, following an anti-British revolt in Iraq, he advocated offering the Germans use of French airfields in Syria, but in July 1941 Syria was invaded by Allied forces, which put paid to any such scheme. Darlan also signed a series of protocols allowing the Germans to use airfields and other facilities in the unoccupied zone of France.

Darlan resigned from government in April 1942, following the return to power of Pierre Laval as premier, but remained in charge of the Vichy armed forces. At the time of the Allied landings in North Africa Darlan was High Commissioner for the colonies there. General Mark Clark made contact with him and promised to recognize his claim to be head of the French government, but luckily for the future of inter-Allied relations Darlan was assassinated by a young French student, Fernand Bonnier de la Chapelle, on Christmas Eve 1942.

Admiral Darlan made no secret of the fact that he hated the British, and might have made life very difficult for the Allies had he not been assassinated. (ECP Armées)

General Charles de Gaulle
French Statesman

Charles de Gaulle's principal concern was to salvage 'the honour of France'. (ECP Armées)

On 28 May, 1940, with the Dunkirk evacuation in full swing and German Panzer divisions on the Channel coast, a counter-attack was launched against the German southern flank by the French 4th Armoured Division, coming up from the Aisne river. The assault enjoyed some success, but on the 30th it was stopped by withering German fire, and with most of its tanks destroyed it was withdrawn to rest and refit. A few days later, the divisional commander departed for Paris, having just been appointed Under-Secretary of State at the War office. His name was General Charles de Gaulle.

Born in 1890, Charles de Gaulle graduated from the St-Cyr Military College and served in France during World War I until being wounded and taken prisoner at Verdun in 1916. Between the wars he was responsible for a number of publications, largely ignored at the time, advocating the formation of a mechanized battle corps. In May 1940 de Gaulle was a colonel, and when the German Blitzkrieg began he was given command of two scratch armoured brigades, which valiantly engaged German forces thrusting into France over the River Meuse. A few days later, he was promoted general and given command of the 4th Armoured Division.

Strongly opposed to the Franco-German armistice, de Gaulle flew to London, and in a famous radio broadcast on 18 June he declared that 'France has lost a battle, but not the war'. Establishing his headquarters in London, he set about organizing the Free French Forces. In 1943, after the Allies had secured North Africa, he became co-president with General Giraud of the French Committee of National Liberation, but in June 1944 he forced Giraud out of the governing body, which he then proclaimed the Provisional Government of France. This instrument was recognized by the Allies after de Gaulle made his triumphant entry into Paris on 26 August 1944, after the city had been liberated by the French Resistance and General Leclerc's 2nd Armoured Division.

In November 1945 de Gaulle was elected provisional President of France, but resigned after only a few months after extreme left-wing elements virtually took over the new government. In 1947 he became head of a new party (Rally of the French People), with the aim of ending internal strife. He retired in 1953 to his country home at Colombey-les-deux-Eglises, but in 1958, after the revolt in Algeria, he became Prime Minister and drew up a new constitution that strengthened the power of the President. He himself became President of the new Fifth Republic in 1959, and much of his time in office was devoted to restoring France to her position as a world power. In May 1968, however, student riots and a wave of strikes throughout France combined to disrupt his administration. In the following year he was defeated on a referendum on constitutional reform, and resigned. He played no further part in public affairs, and died in 1970.

Lieutenant-General Sir Miles Dempsey
British Army

Born in New Brighton, Cheshire, in 1896, Miles Christopher Dempsey first saw service as a young officer in France during World War I, and in 1919–20 he was on active service in Mesopotamia (Iraq), where there was serious unrest following the collapse of the Ottoman Empire. Promotion came slowly for Dempsey during the inter-war years; by 1930 he was still only a lieutenant-colonel, but his advancement thereafter was rapid. In 1940 he commanded the 13th Infantry Brigade in France; this formation moved into Belgium when the Germans attacked in May, and subsequently played a key part in the fighting retreat that ended in the evacuation of the British Expeditionary Force from Dunkirk.

In 1941 Dempsey was made acting major-general, and in 1942 acting lieutenant-general. After the Battle of El Alamein he joined the Eighth Army as commander of XIII Corps, which he led during the advance to Tunisia and later in the invasion of Sicily and southern Italy. In 1944 he was appointed to the command of the British Second Army, which formed part of 21st Army Group under Field Marshal Montgomery during the invasion of France and the subsequent drive through north-west Europe. In August 1944, after the heavy fighting in the battle for Caen, Dempsey led his army expertly in a series of well-executed moves, the most important of which was a thrust across the Seine east of Rouen to trap the remnants of the German Seventh Army. Dempsey's spearheads reached Amiens on 31 August, having covered the seventy miles from the Seine in two days and a night. Crossing the Somme, they then drove on swiftly past Arras and Lille to the Belgian frontier, behind the back of the German Fifteenth Army on the Pas de Calais coast.

In March 1945 Dempsey's Second Army crossed the Rhine at Wesel, having fought its way through Holland and the Reichswald. It reached the Elbe on 24 April and pushed on to capture Hamburg on 3 May, five days before the German surrender.

With hostilities in Europe over, Dempsey was sent to Burma to succeed General Sir William Slim as commander of the Fourteenth Army. He returned to England in 1947. He died at Yattendon, Berkshire, in 1969, after a long and productive retirement.

A fine general, Sir Miles Dempsey commanded the British Second Army with great skill in its advance through north-west Europe. (National Archives)

General Jacob Devers
US Army

Commanding the 6th Army Group in its drive into Germany from the French Riviera, General Devers made an immense contribution to the Allied war effort. (National Archives)

Born in 1887, Jacob Devers graduated from the US Military Academy, West Point, in 1905 and was commissioned into the artillery as a 2nd lieutenant. His early assignments took him to Hawaii, France and Germany in the 1920s. He subsequently graduated from the Command and General Staff College and the Army War College, and continued his assignments with artillery units until 1939, when he was appointed Chief of Staff to the Panama Canal Department.

In August 1941 Devers, then the youngest major-general in the US Army, assumed command of the Armored Force at Fort Knox, taking over from Major-General Adna R. Chaffee, the 'father' of the US armoured forces. Under Devers's command the US armoured strength grew from two divisions to sixteen, with 63 separate tank battalions. Devers also arranged for light aircraft to be attached to the divisional artillery for spotting purposes. Following his service at Fort Knox, Devers was sent to England as Commander, US Land Forces in Europe, in which capacity he supervised the American build-up in Britain in 1942. After the Allied landings in North Africa he was appointed to command the US forces in that theatre of operations. He later became Deputy Commander-in-Chief, Allied Force Headquarters, and Deputy Supreme Commander, Mediterranean Theatre, under Sir Henry Maitland Wilson.

In August 1944 General Devers directed Operation Dragoon, the Allied landings in southern France, and commanded the 6th Army Group, comprising American and Free French divisions, in the subsequent drive to the German border and into Germany itself. He later commanded the 12th Army Group, and after hostilities were over he was appointed Commander of the Army Ground Forces. In that post, he continued the pioneering work he had begun at Fort Knox by organizing helicopter-borne army units, a concept first put into practice in the Korean War (and, incidentally, by the British forces in Malaya at about the same time).

General Jacob Devers, whose contribution to the Allied war effort was immense, retired in 1949 and made his home in Washington, where he died on 15 October 1979. He is buried in Arlington National Cemetery.

Admiral Karl Doenitz
German Navy

Born in Berlin-Grenau on 16 September 1891, Karl Doenitz enlisted in the Imperial German Navy as a cadet in 1910 and was commissioned in 1913. After initial service on a cruiser in the Mediterranean, he transferred to the submarine service in 1916. On 4 October 1918, his submarine, the *UB.68*, was scuttled in the Ionian Sea after being damaged by British warships, and he was taken prisoner, being released in July 1919. He remained in the post-war German Navy, and in 1935, now a Kapitän, he was placed in charge of the new Kriegsmarine's submarine service.

Doenitz stated that he needed 1,000 submarines if Germany was to have any hope of countering Britain's sea power, but by 1939 he still had only 57, of which 22 were seagoing craft. In fact, for a period of several months beginning in June 1940, the Italians had more submarines operating in the Atlantic than did the Germans. As German submarine strength increased, however, Doenitz was able to apply the 'wolfpack' concept, in which the U-boats, operating in groups, were deployed to various ocean areas to ambush Allied convoys. Early in 1942, he also implemented Operation Paukenschlag (Drumbeat), a U-boat offensive against American mercantile traffic in the western Atlantic.

In January 1943, Doenitz succeeded Admiral Erich Raeder as Commander-in-Chief of the Navy. He continued in command of the U-boat fleet, which, after inflicting heavy losses on the Allies in 1942, was now being progressively destroyed by Allied air and sea power. In September 1943, heavily armed U-boats equipped with radar warning receivers began a renewed offensive against Allied shipping, but in eight weeks 25 were sunk, and in that period they destroyed only nine merchant ships. Losses became increasingly grievous, until in 1944 they reached the point when almost one submarine was being destroyed for every Allied ship sunk.

Doenitz planned to renew his offensive at the end of 1944 with a new U-boat, the Type XXI, but construction was frustrated by the Allied bombing campaign and it never became operational. Other U-boat types fought on until the very last days of the war, but by this time the Battle of the Atlantic had long since been won by the Allies.

Early in 1945, Doenitz masterminded the seaborne evacuation of over two million German servicemen and civilians from pockets along the Baltic in the path of the advancing Russians. On 1 May 1945, he succeeded Adolf Hitler, who had committed suicide the day before, as Führer, and after forming a new government he negotiated the surrender of all German forces.

Admiral Doenitz, who lost both his sons in action during the war, was sentenced to ten years' imprisonment at the Nuremberg War Crimes Tribunal. He died on 24 December 1980.

Admiral Karl Doenitz and members of his staff leaving his headquarters at Lorient, France, in 1942. (author's collection)

Marshal of the Royal Air Force Lord Douglas of Kirtleside Royal Air Force

William Sholto Douglas pictured during his time as AOC-in-C, RAF Fighter Command. (IWM)

William Sholto Douglas was born in Headington, Oxfordshire, on 23 December 1893 and educated at Lincoln College, Oxford. At the outbreak of World War I he was commissioned into the Royal Artillery, but in 1915 he transferred to the Royal Flying Corps, serving as an observer before training as a pilot. He eventually commanded No. 43 Squadron, equipped with Sopwith 1½ Strutters, which suffered appalling casualties in the April battles of 1917. Severely injured in a take-off accident, Douglas made a full recovery and returned to France to command No. 84 Squadron, equipped with SE.5As, in September. While commanding this unit Douglas gained at least six victories, and was awarded a DFC to add to his MC, which he had earned in 1916.

Douglas ended the war as a lieutenant-colonel, and left to RAF to become a commercial pilot. He rejoined the Service in 1920 at the instigation of Sir Hugh Trenchard, the first post-war Chief of Air Staff, and rose rapidly up the promotion ladder. By the outbreak of World War II in September 1939 he was an air vice-marshal, Assistant Chief of Air Staff, and in 1940 he was promoted air marshal, with the appointment of Deputy Chief of Air Staff. In November 1940 he succeeded Air Chief Marshal Sir Hugh Dowding as AOC-in-C, RAF Fighter Command. Whereas Dowding had conducted Fighter Command in a very successful defensive role during the Battle of Britain, Douglas now saw it go over to the offensive in the first stages of an ongoing operation that would eventually lead to complete Allied air superiority over north-west Europe.

On leaving Fighter Command Douglas became AOC-in-C Middle East Air Command, with the rank of air chief marshal, and in January 1944 he became AOC-in-C Coastal Command. He took over at a significant phase of the Battle of the Atlantic, when the Germans were beginning to deploy Schnorkel-equipped U-boats, making them more difficult to detect because they no longer needed to surface to recharge their batteries. It was also a period when the newly-formed Coastal Command strike wings were beginning to inflict serious losses on the enemy's coastal convoys. For the final year of the war, Coastal Command, under Douglas's leadership, kept up a merciless offensive against the German Navy, both below and above the waves.

After the war, Douglas was appointed Commander-in-Chief, British Air Forces in Germany, and in 1946 he was promoted Marshal of the Royal Air Force, the highest rank attainable. His final year of service included the duties of Military Governor, and in that capacity he signed the death warrant of former Luftwaffe commander Hermann Goering, whom he had once met in combat over Flanders. In the event, Goering cheated the hangman by taking poison.

On leaving the RAF, Douglas became a director of BOAC, and from 1949 he served as managing director of British European Airways. He died in London on 31 October 1969.

Air Chief Marshal Sir Hugh Dowding
Royal Air Force

Air Chief Marshal Sir Hugh Dowding (left), with Group Captain Douglas Bader, the famous 'legless ace'. (via Phil Jarrett)

Hugh Caswall Tremenheere Dowding was born at Moffat, Scotland, on 24 April 1882, the son of a preparatory school headmaster, and was educated at Winchester School and the Royal Military Academy, Woolwich. He served with the Royal Artillery in Gibraltar, Ceylon, Hong Kong and India, and on returning to Britain he learned to fly. On obtaining his licence he joined the Royal Flying Corps, with which he went to France on the outbreak of World War I. In 1916 he was promoted major and given command of No. 16 Squadron, an army co-operation unit which was equipped with BE.2cs and which suffered heavy losses during the Battle of the Somme. Dowding clashed with General Hugh Trenchard, the RFC's C-in-C, over the need to rest exhausted pilots; as a result he was sent home, and although promoted rapidly to the rank of brigadier-general, he saw no more active service in World War I. After the war, promotion came steadily; by 1933 he was an air marshal, and received a knighthood in the following year. As the Air Member for Research and Development, he was one of the first to recognize the need for all-metal monoplane fighters, and it was on his authority that the first radar experiments with aircraft were carried out. In July 1936 he became the first Air Officer Commanding-in-Chief of the newly created RAF Fighter Command, and in 1937 he reached the rank of air chief marshal. In the summer of 1939, at the age of 57, he was due for retirement, but was persuaded to stay in his post.

In May 1940, Dowding persuaded the new Prime Minister, Winston Churchill, against sending further RAF fighter reinforcements to France, where the Allied cause was lost. Although he was criticized by other air commanders for an apparent lack of aggression during the Battle of Britain, he had an instinctive understanding of the essentials of air warfare. He was the chief inspiration of the ground control system, extending from his HQ at Bentley Priory to the fighter airfields, that was essential to the RAF's survival. Once the battle began, he never lost sight of the need to be able to fight again the next day and the next week, whatever the temptations and pressures to risk everything on the battle of the moment; and his policy of resting his front-line fighter squadrons at intervals paid enormous dividends.

On being relieved of his post in November 1940, Dowding was sent on a special mission to the United States on behalf of the Ministry of Aircraft Production. He retired from the RAF in July 1942, and was honoured with a baronetcy in the following year.

Lord Dowding was nicknamed 'Stuffy' by his subordinates, and the name no doubt summed up his character, at least in part. An unyielding man to the point of stubbornness, his conduct of Fighter Command in its finest hour saved Britain. In his later years he became a spiritualist, and claimed to be in touch with some of the young fighter pilots who had lost their lives. He died on 15 February 1970.

General Ira C. Eaker
US Army Air Force

Ira Clarence Eaker, later to become famous as the man who forged the US Eighth Air Force – the 'Mighty Eighth' – in World War II, was born in Llano, Texas, on 13 April 1896. He originally served as an infantry officer, transferring to the US Air Service in 1917. He first came to prominence in January 1929 when, together with co-pilot Carl Spaatz, he set up an endurance record of more than 150 hours aloft in a Fokker C-2A trimotor, an exploit for which he and Spaatz were awarded the DFC. Eaker's position as a first-class aviator was consolidated in 1936, when he crossed the American continent from coast to coast relying solely on the new gyroscopic 'blind flying' aids recently developed by Elmer Sperry.

Promoted brigadier-general in 1942, Eaker was given command of the US Eighth Army Air Force, which was beginning to form in England. Eaker was convinced that the strategic bombing of Germany could be successfully accomplished in daylight by large formations of bombers flying in mutually defensive boxes, and on 17 August 1942 he personally led the Eighth AF's first raid on Europe, an attack by 12 B-17s on marshalling yards at Rouen. When the Allied leaders and their chiefs of staff met at Casablanca in January 1943 to discuss the future conduct of the war, it was decided to implement Eaker's daylight bombing plans, while RAF Bomber Command continued with its night offensive. The daylight offensive faltered badly in the summer of 1943, when unescorted bombers began deep-penetration raids into Germany and suffered appalling losses, but the tide began to turn a few months later, when the North American P-51 Mustang long-range escort fighter became available in numbers.

In September 1943 Eaker was promoted lieutenant-general and placed in overall command of the US Army Air Forces in Britain, and assisted in the planning of Operation Overlord before being reassigned to command the Mediterranean Allied Air Forces. In this capacity he conducted the air offensive against Germany from bases in Italy, and in August 1944 commanded the air formations covering the Allied landings on the south coast of France and supporting the subsequent drive inland by General Devers's 6th Army Group.

General Eaker relinquished command of the Mediterranean Allied Air Forces in March 1945 and became Deputy Commanding General of the United States Army Air Force, remaining in this post until his retirement in 1947. For the next ten years he was vice-president of the Hughes Tool Corporation.

General Ira C. Eaker, one of the most formidable architects of air power, died on 6 August 1987.

General Ira C. Eaker was the instrument that forged the US Eighth Air Force into an instrument of formidable striking power. (National Archives)

37

General Dwight D. Eisenhower
US Army

Dwight D. Eisenhower, Supreme Commander of the Allied forces that stormed through Hitler's 'Atlantic Wall' to victory in Europe. (National Archives)

Dwight David Eisenhower, the man who was destined to become one of the most famous names of the twentieth century as soldier and statesman, was born in Texas in 1890 and brought up in Abilene, Kansas. A graduate of the US Military Academy, West Point, in 1915, his early military assignments showed him to have outstanding ability as a staff officer. His organizational ability saw him shuttled from one military establishment to another in the United States during World War I, until on 14 October 1918 he was given what he had always desired: a combat command. His orders were to take charge of a US armoured unit in France, effective 28 November 1918.

Unfortunately for Eisenhower, the Armistice came into effect on 11 November and he remained a staff officer. In 1922 he was assigned to the defence of the Panama Canal Zone, serving under General Fox Connor. He later worked in the War Department, and from 1933 to 1935 he served in the Philippines under General Douglas MacArthur. In 1940 he commanded an infantry battalion at Fort Lewis, Washington State, and in 1941 he was appointed Chief of Staff to General Walter Krueger of the Third Army.

Soon after the attack on Pearl Harbor, Eisenhower was promoted brigadier-general and placed in charge of domestic planning for the American war effort in the Far East. In 1942, the US Army Chief of Staff, General George C. Marshall, appointed him US Commander in the European theatre of operations, and in November 1942 he was put in charge of Operation Torch, the Anglo-American landings in Morocco and Algeria. The success of this operation, and President Roosevelt's desire to retain a controlling influence in the European war, led to Eisenhower's appointment, despite opposition, as Supreme Commander Allied Forces in Europe. As such, he oversaw the preparation and execution of Operation Overlord, the Allied landings in Normandy, for which he devised a system of unified command in which staff officers of many nations generally co-operated effectively. As a commander he had many virtues, not least of which were his amiable disposition and coolness in adversity. After Normandy, Eisenhower insisted on the Allied forces advancing on a broad and unified front, instead of attempting a rapid thrust into Germany on a narrow front; the wisdom of this policy has long been debated, but, given the ability of the German Army to reorganize itself with amazing speed and efficiency after a defeat, he was probably right.

After the war, Eisenhower became President of Columbia University, and in 1951 he was appointed NATO Supreme Allied Commander, Europe (SACEUR). Between 1953 and 1961 he served two consecutive terms as President of the United States. Suffering with heart problems, he retired to his farm in Gettysburg in 1961, and died there on 28 March 1969.

General Bernard Freyberg
British Army

General Freyberg possessed personal courage, as well as considerable powers of leadership. He came close to frustrating the airborne assault on Crete.

A fighting leader of great personal courage, Bernard Freyberg was born in London in 1889 but was raised in New Zealand. In 1911 he qualified as a dentist, and in 1912 he was commissioned into the New Zealand Territorial Army. In 1913, growing tired of dentistry, he abruptly changed jobs and became a stoker on board ship, working his passage to England. He was in London when World War I erupted in August 1914, and – thanks to a chance meeting with the First Lord of the Admiralty, Winston Churchill – he was commissioned into the Hood Battalion of the newly formed Royal Naval Division, which went into action in the defence of Antwerp.

Freyberg subsequently fought at Gallipoli, where he won the DSO. Transferred to the Western Front, he led the Hood Battalion in a series of spirited actions on the River Ancre, and in November 1916, for his courage in refusing to leave the battalion despite having been wounded four times in 24 hours, he was awarded the Victoria Cross. In April 1917 he was promoted to the rank of brigadier, at the age of 27 the youngest in the British Army. By the end of the war he had been wounded nine times and had received three Bars to his DSO. He was now in command of a division, the 29th Infantry.

Between the wars Freyberg served in various staff and command posts until, at the outbreak of

World War II, he was placed in command of the New Zealand Expeditionary Force in North Africa, leading it through its early desert campaigns. He was then sent to command the remnants of the expedition to Greece, who had withdrawn to the island of Crete, and his leadership there was much criticized when the defenders were overwhelmed by German airborne forces in May 1941. He returned to the desert to command the 2nd New Zealand Division, and was badly wounded at the battle of Minqar Quaim in 1942. On his recovery he returned to active service, first in the desert and then in Italy, where he played a key part in the assault on Monte Cassino. He continued to command the New Zealand forces in Italy until May 1945, when his troops entered Trieste.

Freyberg ended the war as a lieutenant-general, and in 1946 was appointed Governor-General of New Zealand. In 1951 he was created Baron of Wellington and Munstead. He died in 1963.

German pioneers attacking New Zealand positions during the battle for Crete. (via J. R. Cavanagh)

General Freyberg in the Western Desert, 1942. (IWM)

General Maurice Gamelin
French Army

Going to the aid of their French allies, troops of the British Expeditionary Force march through Paris, September 1939.
(author's collection)

The son of a general, Maurice Gamelin was born in Paris on 20 September 1872. In 1891 he graduated top of his class at the St Cyr Military Academy, and was commissioned into the 1st Regiment of Algerian Tirailleurs. In 1906 he was promoted captain and selected by General Joffre, the French Army commander, to serve as his aide. He later commanded a chasseur battalion, and was recalled to Joffre's staff on the outbreak of World War I. Promoted brigadier-general in 1916, he served with distinction throughout the war, and in January 1930 he was appointed Deputy Chief of the general Staff under General Maxime Weygand. In the following year he was made Inspector-General of the Army. When Weygand retired as Chief of the General Staff in 1935, Gamelin replaced him. The post should have gone to another senior officer, General Alphonse Georges, but the French Prime Minister considered him too right wing and appointed Gamelin instead, Georges being given command of the Northern Army Zone.

It was Gamelin who, in September 1939, authorized an offensive on the Saar Front, a few days after the Germans invaded Poland. In London and Paris, newspapers hailed the offensive as an overwhelming success, but in fact it was nothing of the sort. The Germans resisted the offensive fiercely and the French suffered heavy losses; their only gains were a few villages which the Germans had decided to abandon for tactical reasons.

The flaws in Gamelin's leadership were revealed in the days after 10 May 1940, when the French armies crumbled under the onslaught of the German Panzer divisions. For the first three days of the Blitzkrieg, Gamelin refused to authorize the French air force to attack the tightly packed enemy columns advancing through the Ardennes 'for fear of reprisals'. On 17 May, a broken man, he was sacked by Premier Daladier and replaced by Marshal Weygand, brought out of retirement. For France, it was too late. Three days later, the German tanks reached the Channel coast.

In September 1940 Maurice Gamelin was arrested by the Vichy authorities and held in France before being deported to Germany in 1943 and imprisoned in Buchenwald. He was liberated by the Americans in May 1945, and died on 18 April 1958.

General James Gavin
US Army

The child who would one day rise to be a three-star general had an inauspicious start to life, born the illegitimate son of an Irish immigrant girl in 1907 and spending his early months in a New York orphanage. He was eventually adopted by Martin and Mary Gavin, and spent his youth in the tough environment of the Pennsylvania coalfields. At the age of 17 he escaped from it by enlisting in the US Army as a private, and showed such promise that he was awarded a cadetship to the US Military Academy, West Point. There, he made a thorough study of history's greatest generals and their tactics and strategy, and became attracted to the principles of mobile warfare. As the most mobile troops were airborne forces, it was natural that he should also be attracted to this concept, and it was as an airborne commander that he achieved fame, leading the 82nd Airborne Division – formed from the 82nd 'All American' Division on 5 August 1942 – on airborne operations in Sicily and Italy in 1943, by which time he had reached the rank of brigadier-general.

On the first night of the Allied invasion of Normandy, 5–6 June 1944, the 82nd Airborne, although badly scattered during their drop, took the town of Sainte-Mère-Eglise and guarded river crossings on the flank of the Utah Beach landing area. After the Normandy operations Gavin was made a major-general at the age of 37, making him the youngest officer to hold this rank since General Custer. In September 1944 Gavin dropped into Holland with his division during Operation Market Garden, capturing the river crossings at Nijmegen. The 82nd subsequently fought its way into Germany.

Nicknamed 'Jumping Jim', General Gavin was Head of Army Research and Development during the 1950s. He strongly opposed President Eisenhower's defence policy because of its dependence on nuclear weapons, and retired in 1958. During the Kennedy administration (1961–3) he became the US Ambassador to France; later in the 1960s he became an outspoken critic of the war in Vietnam, which he believed should be ended by any means available. General Gavin wrote a number of books, including his autobiographical *On to Berlin*, before his death in 1990.

General James ('Jumping Jim') Gavin was the youngest major-general in the US Army since George Armstrong Custer. (National Archives)

General Henri Honoré Giraud
French Army

Born in 1879, Henri Giraud was a graduate of St Cyr. He served in World War I and later in the Moroccan campaign of 1925–6. At the outbreak of World War II he was in command of the French Seventh Army, stationed on the Franco-Belgian border, When the German attack began on 10 May 1940 this formation moved up to confront the Germans in Holland, and in less than a week it had virtually ceased to exist as a fighting force, having been completely outfought and outmanoeuvred. In the meantime, on 15 May Giraud had been ordered to take command of the Ninth Army, but instead of the intact units which he had been led to expect, he found himself in command of an army which had been virtually destroyed, many of its units existing only on paper.

With no hope of forming a cohesive resistance, Giraud ordered the remnants of his command to re-form on the Sambre-Oise Canal line. Despite all the signs, he appeared blind to the fact that everything was lost; he continued to organize his divisions as though the shattered remnants of his force were still fully equipped combat units, making plans for counter-attacks with forces that no longer existed. His final delusions were destroyed on 19 May, when he and members of his staff were captured by German troops.

In April 1942 Giraud succeeded in escaping, and made his way to Gibraltar, where he joined the Free French forces. He took part in the Allied landings in North Africa, and when Admiral Darlan, the French commander in North Africa, was assassinated in December, Giraud assumed his duties as High Commissioner. Despite being extremely active on behalf of the Free French, organizing the army that liberated Corsica in September 1943, he soon came into conflict with General de Gaulle, and although serving with him on the French Committee of National Liberation, was quickly removed from office, being virtually compelled to resign by de Gaulle on 8 April 1944. General Giraud died in 1949.

General Giraud campaigned vigorously on behalf of the Free French cause, but came into conflict with General Charles de Gaulle. (ECP Armées)

Reichsmarschall Hermann Goering
German Air Force and National Socialist Politician

A talented pilot, and a World War I flying ace, Hermann Goering commanded the Richthofen Jagdgeschwader in 1918. (Bundesarchiv)

Hermann Wilhelm Goering was born at Rosenheim, Bavaria, on 12 January 1893. Commissioned into the Imperial Army as a Leutnant in March 1912, he fought as an infantry officer from the beginning of World War I until October 1914, when he transferred to the Imperial German Air Service, flying initially as an artillery observer. In 1915 he retrained as a pilot and flew reconnaissance missions with Abteilung 5 before joining a fighter unit, Jagdstaffel 27. In May 1918 he was awarded the Pour le Mérite, Germany's highest decoration for gallantry, following his 21st aerial victory. In July he was appointed commander of the celebrated Richthofen Jagdgeschwader, remaining in that position until the Armistice.

After the war, he engaged in a series of aviation enterprises in Germany and Sweden. An early confidant of Adolf Hitler, he joined the new National Socialist Party, and in 1923 he played an active part in Hitler's abortive Putsch in Munich, fleeing to Sweden when it failed. In 1928, following a government amnesty, he returned to Germany and again became active in politics. In May 1928 he was elected to the Reichstag, and became its president in 1932. In 1933, following the establishment of the National Socialist government, he was appointed to a number of important posts, including that of State Minister for Air, in which capacity he created the Luftwaffe. A staunch advocate of air power as a decisive factor in war, Goering developed revolutionary ideas of tactical air support, but proved less able to maintain the air force on a sound economic basis. As Commander-in-Chief of the Luftwaffe, he was promoted to Generalfeldmarschall in 1938, and in 1939 he was designated as Hitler's successor, a distinction that made him the second most powerful man in Germany. In 1940 he was given the unique rank of Reichsmarschall.

Initially an immensely popular and charismatic figure, his popularity began to wane after the failure of the Luftwaffe to subdue the RAF in the Battle of Britain, and it declined still more after it proved unable to supply the German Sixth Army at Stalingrad, as he had promised it would. Earlier, he had proclaimed that if enemy aircraft flew over the Reich, people could call him Meyer (a Jewish name), but by 1943 Germany was being attacked by day and night, giving the lie to another of his bombastic promises. He began to withdraw from public life more and more, and when he did intervene in the running of the Luftwaffe his influence was often harmful, his poor strategic judgement inhibiting the air force from making the most of a huge increase in aircraft production in 1944.

On 23 April 1945, following a belated attempt to wrest power from Hitler, he was dismissed from all his posts. In May he surrendered to American troops. At Nuremberg, he was tried on charges of conspiracy, crimes against peace, general war crimes and crimes against humanity. Convicted of all four, he was sentenced to death by hanging, but two hours before the sentence was due to be carried out, on 15 October 1946, he committed suicide by swallowing a cyanide capsule concealed in a hollow tooth.

Goering's 'wonder bomber', a Junkers Ju 88, about to take off on a mission against England in 1940.

Field Marshal Viscount Gort
British Army

Troops of Lord Gort's British Expeditionary Force on their way to France, September 1939. Note the World War I style uniforms. (author's collection)

John Standish Prendergast Vereker Gort, the son of the 5th Viscount Gort, was born at Hamsterly Hall, County Durham, England, in 1886 and succeeded his father as 6th Viscount in 1902. Educated at Harrow and the Royal Military College, Woolwich, he was commissioned into the Grenadier Guards in 1905. During World War I Gort was mentioned in dispatches nine times and won the Distinguished Service Order and two Bars and the Military Cross, and on 27 September 1918 he was awarded the Victoria Cross for an action at the Canal du Nord in which he led his men in a successful assault, despite being twice wounded.

After the war, Gort taught at the Military Staff College and was promoted colonel in 1925. During the inter-war years he served as Commander of the Guards Brigade (1930–2), Director of Military Training in India (1932–6), and Commandant of the Staff College (1936–9). He was made a full general in 1937, in which year he was also appointed Chief of the Imperial General Staff. In 1939 he was made Commander-in-Chief of the British Expeditionary Force (BEF), which deployed to France at the outbreak of World War II. In the crucial weeks following the German assault on the West, which began on 10 May 1940, he showed superb generalship in organizing the orderly fighting retreat of the BEF to Dunkirk, using a great deal of initiative in authorizing the evacuation of non-combatants at an early stage to clear the way for the final evacuation of the fighting troops. On 30 May, to prevent his possible capture by the Germans, Prime Minister Winston Churchill ordered him back to England.

On his return, Gort was appointed ADC to King George VI, and in 1941–2 he was made Governor of Gibraltar. This was followed, in 1942, by his appointment as Governor of Malta, at a time when the island was undergoing its time of greatest peril. He held the post until 1944, when he was appointed High Commissioner to Palestine.

Field Marshal Viscount Gort died in March 1946. He was neither a strategist nor a deep military thinker, but he had great courage, and the ability to see a clear road through a tangled web of confusion that might have ensnared other, less forthright military commanders. He never received the credit which was his due.

Generaloberst Heinz Guderian
German Army

Born on 17 June 1888 into a West Prussian military family, Heinz Guderian was commissioned into the 10th Hanoverian Jäger Battalion in 1907. In 1913 he was at the Kriegsakademie (Military College), and throughout World War I he served as a staff officer, except for a single tour of duty as a battalion commander on the Western Front in 1917. After the war he served in the Freikorps on the Eastern Front and in several staff appointments, chiefly in the Motorized Troops Directorate, Germany's cover organization for the development of armoured warfare. In 1927 he was promoted Major, and in 1933 Oberst. In 1934 he was appointed Chief of Staff to the Panzer Command, in 1935 he became General Officer Commanding 2 Panzer Command, and in 1938, as a Generalleutnant, he was appointed to the command of XVI Army Corps. In the same year he was promoted general, and appointed Chief of Mobile Troops.

Guderian commanded XIX Corps during the invasion of Poland in 1939, and in the assault on the West in May and June 1940. He was then given command of a Panzer Group and promoted Generaloberst. In 1941 he became commander of the Second Panzer Army, which he led with great brilliance in Russia until he was relieved of his command in December 1941, thanks to the enmity of Feldmarschall von Kluge, who persuaded Hitler that Guderian had not carried out his mission after the Germans failed to take Moscow. After a period in retirement he was made Inspector-General of Armoured Troops, and then, after the attempt on Hitler's life in July 1944, Chief of the General Staff. After frequent disagreements with Hitler on the conduct of the war, he was dismissed on the grounds of ill-health on 28 March 1945. He was taken prisoner by the Americans, and it was decided that he had played no part in Nazi war crimes.

Guderian's methods were unorthodox for a man of his rank; when in action, he would leave his headquarters at dawn in an armoured car, with a signals officer, a radio and an Enigma cipher machine, and would direct operations at the front while still keeping in touch with his HQ. His legacy is that he created the Panzerwaffe, the powerful armoured force which remains at the tactical heart of modern armies today, and laid the foundations for its effective employment.

Heinz Guderian died in Schwangau on 14 May 1954.

Heinz Guderian's legacy to military history was that he created the Panzerwaffe, the armoured force which is still the nucleus of modern armies. (Bundesarchiv)

Fleet Admiral William F. Halsey
US Navy

Admiral Halsey directed US naval operations off the Philippines and in Japanese home waters in 1944–5. *(US Navy)*

Division Two in USS *Yorktown* and then Carrier Division One in *Saratoga*, and in 1940, now a vice-admiral, he became Commander, Aircraft Carrier Battle Force. After America's entry into the war, he led the early carrier air strikes on the Marshall and Gilbert Islands in February 1942, and in April he commanded the carrier task force operating in support of the famous raid on Tokyo by B-25 bombers, launched from the USS *Hornet* and led by Colonel Jimmy Doolittle.

From October 1942 to June 1944, Halsey commanded the Allied South Pacific Naval Forces with the rank of admiral. Subsequently, as Third Fleet Commander, he directed naval operations off the Philippines, playing a prominent role in the Battle of Leyte Gulf, and in Japanese home waters. On 2 September 1945, the Japanese surrender was signed aboard his flagship, the USS *Missouri*.

On 11 December 1945, Halsey was made Fleet Admiral, the fourth and last officer to achieve this rank. He retired in 1947, and served on the boards of various commercial enterprises until his death on 16 August 1959.

One of the most aggressive naval commanders of World War II, William Frederick Halsey was born in Elizabeth, New Jersey, on 30 October 1882, the son of a US Navy captain. In 1900 he entered the US Naval Academy, where, although poor in scholarship, he distinguished himself as a leader and in sporting activities. On graduating in 1904 he was assigned to the USS *Missouri*, and in 1906, having completed the required two years at sea, he was commissioned as an ensign. Although his initial service was in battleships, Halsey spent most of the next 25 years in destroyers, his seagoing duty interspersed with duty ashore. During the 1920s, for example, he served as Naval Attaché to the US Embassies in Berlin, Christiana (Norway), Stockholm and Copenhagen.

In 1934, his career took a different turn when he reported for flight training at the US Naval Air Station, Pensacola. Graduating in May 1935, he was given command of the aircraft-carrier USS *Saratoga*. This was followed by a year in command of Pensacola Air Station. In 1938, when he reached flag rank, Halsey was given command of Carrier

Halsey's Japanese opponents at Leyte: Admirals Kurita (above), who withdrew prematurely and destroyed his chances of victory, and Ozawa (right), the cool, gallant commander of the carrier task force.

46

Marshal of the Royal Air Force Sir Arthur T. Harris Royal Air Force

Air Chief Marshal Sir Arthur Harris and members of his staff examining damage assessment photographs after an attack. (RAF)

Few commanders, at least on the Allied side, have inspired as much controversy as Air Chief Marshal Sir Arthur Harris, whose area bombing policy in World War II devastated Germany's cities.

Born in Cheltenham, England, on 13 April 1892, Arthur Travers Harris went to Rhodesia as an 18-year-old in 1910 and became involved in various commercial ventures before enlisting in the 1st Rhodesia Regiment in 1914. Returning to India in the following year, he transferred to the Royal Flying Corps, and by the end of the war he was commanding No. 44 Squadron, flying Sopwith Camels. Granted a permanent commission, with the rank of squadron leader, he commanded No. 50 Squadron before embarking on successive tours of duty in India and Iraq. Returning to England in 1925, he was promoted wing commander and given command of No. 58 (Bomber) Squadron, flying Vickers Vimy and Virginia heavy bombers at Worthy Down.

After attending the Army Staff College at Camberley in 1929, Harris spent two years in the Middle East before being appointed Deputy Director, Operations and Intelligence, at the Air Ministry with the rank of group captain. In 1934 he became Head of Plans Branch, Air Ministry, and Air Member, Joint Planning Committee of Imperial Defence; this was followed by promotion to air commodore and command of No. 4 (Bomber) Group. After heading an air mission to the United States in 1938, he spent a year as Air Officer Commanding, RAF Palestine and Transjordan.

In September 1939 Harris, now an air vice-marshal, assumed command of No. 5 (Bomber) Group, comprising ten squadrons of Handley Page Hampden bombers. In November 1940 he was appointed Deputy Chief of Air Staff, and in May 1941, as an acting air marshal, he headed an RAF delegation to the USA. Then, on 22 February 1942, he was confirmed in the appointment with which he would always be associated – Air Officer Commanding-in-Chief, RAF Bomber Command. During the next three years he relentlessly pursued the concept of sustained area bombing, a policy that cost the lives of countless enemy civilians and 55,000 RAF and Commonwealth aircrew. It was not until after the war that his policy was vindicated, when leading Nazis such as armaments minister Albert Speer admitted that area bombing had had a devastating effect on civilian morale. It also had another effect, often ignored by historians: it forced the Germans to disperse their atomic weapons research programme, to the point where it barely continued to function.

In 1946 Harris was promoted to Marshal of the Royal Air Force, and at his own request he was allowed to retire on half pay. The recipient of many honours and awards, he was created a baronet in 1953. He died quietly at home in Goring-on-Thames on 5 April 1984, eight days short of his 92nd birthday. Today, his statue stands beside the RAF Church of St Clement Danes, in London.

General Gotthard Heinrici
German Army

Born in Gumbinnen, Germany, on 25 December 1886, Gotthard Heinrici came from a military family with a tradition extending back to the twelfth century. In 1905 he was commissioned into the 95th Infantry Regiment, and during World War I he served on both fronts. He remained in the army after the end of hostilities, and by the outbreak of World War II he had reached the rank of Generalmajor, commanding the German VII Corps. In April 1940 he assumed command of XII Corps, the formation that broke through France's Maginot Line defences south of Saarbrücken a month later.

During Operation Barbarossa, the German invasion of Russia, Heinrici served under Heinz Guderian in the 2nd Panzer Army. Promoted full general in January 1943, he was given command of the Fourth Army. Heinrici had already proved himself to be an outstanding Panzer commander, and on 15 August 1944 he was appointed to command the 1st Panzer Army, which from then until the end of the war conducted a series of fighting retreats through eastern Europe. In March 1945, with the end of the war in sight, Heinrici was given command of Army Group Vistula, which had previously been commanded by SS Reichsführer Heinrich Himmler.

Heinrici was forced to deal with many crises on the Eastern Front in his various commands, the most serious being the final Soviet assault on Berlin by vastly superior forces under Zhukov and Koniev. A master of the lightning counter-attack, Heinrici used his Panzers to slow down the Russian advance time after time, and used sensible tactics. At the Seelow Heights, for example, a vital strategic position on the approaches to the German capital, he ordered the forward positions to be evacuated so that the enemy barrage would fall on unoccupied land; as soon as the barrage ceased, the Germans reoccupied their positions and brought the Soviet advance to a standstill.

Heinrici believed, correctly, that it was now impossible to defend Berlin, and rejected Hitler's demand that the city be held at all costs. As a consequence, he was relieved of his command on 28 April 1945, just two days before Hitler committed suicide. Heinrici withdrew the remnants of his forces to the Flensburg area, where he was captured by the British on 28 May, three weeks after the German surrender. He was released from captivity on 19 May 1948, and died in Waiblingen (Württemberg) on 13 December 1971.

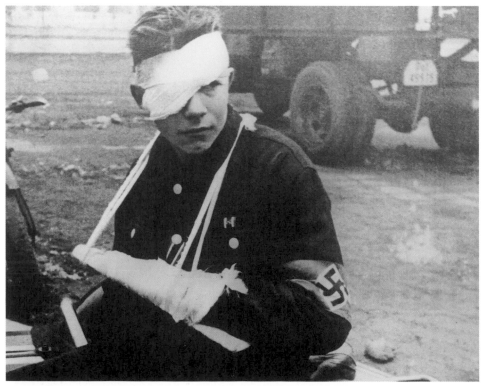

Berlin, April 1945. A wounded Hitler Youth despatch rider seen during the last-ditch defence of the city. (author's collection)

Adolf Hitler
German National Socialist Chancellor

Adolf Hitler takes the salute at a Nazi Party rally in Munich during the 1930s. *(Bundesarchiv)*

The child who was destined to become one of history's most notorious figures was born in Linz, Austria, on 20 April 1889, the son of a minor customs official. In 1909, after the death of his adored mother, he moved to Vienna, living on a modest inheritance and the sale of his water-colours. He moved to Munich in 1913, and in the following year, on the outbreak of World War I, he enlisted in the Bavarian Army. In the course of his service he was both gassed and wounded, and was awarded the Iron Cross, First Class. By the armistice of 1918 he had become convinced that Germany's downfall had been brought about by Jewish and Marxist traitors.

On demobilization, he returned to Munich, where he joined the small German Workers' Party, composed mainly of veterans with strongly nationalistic tendencies. In 1920, the organization was renamed the National Socialist German Workers' Party (Nazi Party), over which Hitler soon gained absolute control. Its ideals attracted some eminently respectable people, one of whom was General Ludendorff, Germany's master strategist in World War I. In 1923, hoping to topple the Bavarian government, Hitler staged his famous 'Putsch' in a Munich Beer Cellar, but his 'storm troopers' were overwhelmed and he himself received a five-year prison sentence. He served only

nine months of it, in Landsberg fortress, and during that time he dictated his book *Mein Kampf* ('My Struggle') to fellow prisoner Rudolf Hess, who was later to become his deputy.

The Nazi Party began to flourish during the world economic depression of 1929, when Hitler's policies for the future of Germany and its economic recovery, delivered with the full force of his brilliant oratory, began to attract an enormous following from all sections of society. In 1932 he ran in the election for President of the Reichstag, but lost to General Paul von Hindenburg. However, by July 1932 the Nazis had become the largest single party in the Reichstag, and when the German Chancellor, Kurt von Schleicher, resigned on 28 January 1933 because of Parliament's inability to cope with growing civil unrest and disorder, Hindenburg appointed Hitler in his place.

Almost immediately, Hitler set about crushing all opposition. The Communist Party was banned after its members were blamed for setting fire to the Reichstag building on 28 February 1933, and a vote was forced through giving Hitler dictatorial powers. Thereafter, political opponents were either murdered or simply 'disappeared', while Jews and left-wing sympathizers were arrested, executed or sent to concentration 49 camps. Hitler had no hesitation in turning on those who had supported his rise to power; Ernst Roehm, head of the SA (Sturmabteilung) was murdered on Hitler's orders, together with many of his brown-shirted bully boys, and after that all members of the German armed forces were required to swear an oath of personal allegiance to Hitler. Following Hindenburg's death in 1934, the positions of president and chancellor were combined in the person of Hitler, who now styled himself Führer (Leader).

The success of Hitler's policies of the 1930s was quite remarkable. He virtually eliminated unemployment by introducing conscription, expanding the army and launching a massive rearmament programme in defiance of the Treaty of Versailles. He embarked on a massive programme of national construction, one aspect of which may still be seen today in the form of the Autobahnen. He annexed Austria and part of Czechoslovakia, while the powers that might have opposed him adopted a policy of appeasement and did nothing. The Italian dictator, Benito Mussolini, became Hitler's ally through the Axis Pact, and both countries sent forces to fight on General Franco's side in the Spanish Civil War. In August 1939 Germany signed a non-aggression pact with the Soviet Union, paving the way for the invasion and occupation of Poland in the following month.

With his eastern flank secure, Hitler launched his assault on the West, invading first Norway and Denmark in April and then France and the Low Countries in May. His plans to invade Britain were thwarted by the defeat of the Luftwaffe at the hands of the RAF, and in June 1941 his forces attacked the USSR in a massive offensive which, although initially incredibly successful, was halted at the gates of Moscow. As a result of the failure in Russia Hitler assumed personal command of German war strategy, but although his armies made further gains in 1942, both in Russia and North Africa, they were stopped and defeated at Stalingrad and El Alamein by the end of the year.

With the United States in the war following the attack on Pearl Harbor by Japan, also a member of the Axis, Germany's position began to deteriorate rapidly, and some German officers, seeking an early end to the war, attempted to kill him by planting a bomb in his HQ in July 1944. The attempt failed, and some 5,000 conspirators or suspected conspirators were executed, some with the utmost brutality.

On 30 April 1945, with the defence of Berlin collapsing under the Russian onslaught, Hitler and his newly married mistress, Eva Braun, committed suicide in his bunker, and their bodies were burned. To the very end, Hitler had persisted in the delusion that Germany would be saved by the deployment of secret weapons. The irony was that the very scientists who could have provided him with those weapons had been forced to flee Germany in the 1930s to escape Nazi persecution, because they were Jewish.

General Courtney Hicks Hodges
US Army

A failure at West Point, Courtney Hodges went on to become one of the finest military commanders of World War II. (National Archives)

Born in Perry, Georgia, on 5 January 1887, Courtney Hodges entered West Point but failed to graduate because of his inability to master mathematics. Nevertheless, he decided to stay in the army, and was eventually commissioned into the 17th Infantry Regiment. In 1916 he accompanied General Pershing's military expedition into Mexico, and in the following year he went to France with the 6th Infantry Regiment, fighting in the battles at St-Mihiel, the Argonne and on the Meuse, and several times distinguishing himself under fire. Between the wars, Hodges held a number of staff and instructional assignments, including one at the US Army Air Corps Tactical School, Langley. He served on liaison duties in Canada, and in 1940, after tours in Washington and the Philippines, he was appointed commandant of the US Infantry Training School, Fort Benning. He was promoted to general officer rank in 1941.

In 1942 he commanded X Corps, and in February 1943 he was given command of the US Southern Defence Area, mostly comprising the Third Army with its HQ at Fort Sam Houston, Texas. He subsequently went with the Third Army to England, and continued to command it until handing over to General George S. Patton in January 1944. He was then appointed deputy to General Omar Bradley, and given command of the US First Army prior to the Allied invasion of Normandy in June 1944. By 13 September, the First Army had penetrated as far as the German Siegfried Line defences and advanced on the town of Aachen, which was captured after a bitter battle. The overall task of the First and Third Armies in the final push into Germany was to drive the Germans out of the Eifel and secure the middle reaches of the Rhine, a task they performed magnificently. It ended when, in April 1945, Hodges' troops linked up with Soviet forces at Torgau, on the river Elbe. Hodges remained in command of the First Army, which returned to the USA and began training for deployment to the Pacific, but the dropping of the atomic bombs made this unnecessary.

General Hodges left the Army in 1949 and died on 16 January 1966.

General Masaharu Homma
Japanese Army

Having studied military strategy and tactics in Great Britain, Masaharu Homma was attached to the British Expeditionary Force on the Western Front as an observer in 1918. In 1927 he became military secretary to Prince Chichibu, younger brother of the Emperor Hirohito. In 1938, he commanded the 27th Division in China, and in 1940 he assumed command of the Army of Formosa.

In November 1941 Homma was given command of the Fourteenth Army and tasked with the invasion of the Philippines. Ten hours after the attack on Pearl Harbor, a series of massive air strikes on air bases in the Philippines wiped out most of the Allies' air power, and after securing Batan Island on 8 December strong Japanese forces landed in northern and southern Luzon, isolating US and Filipino forces around Manila. Meanwhile, Davao was secured on Mindanao, giving the Japanese a stranglehold on the Philippines even before their main forces arrived.

Homma, who had boasted that he could complete the occupation of the Philippines in 45 days, had expected the Allied forces to defend the capital, Manila. Instead, the Allied commander, General Douglas MacArthur, ordered a withdrawal to the Bataan peninsula. In his anxiety to capture Manila, Homma missed the significance of this redeployment, which involved some 80,000 Allied troops. The Fourteenth Army was not sufficiently strong to break through this last line of defence, and by the time Allied resistance collapsed through lack of resupply in April 1942, the Japanese invasion timetable had been thrown into disarray. Homma complained to Tokyo of his inadequate resources and the fatigued condition of his army, and at one point even suspended the assault on Bataan, an unheard-of action on the part of a Japanese general. He was given some replacement divisions, but he was now held in low esteem and was considered to have handled the Filipino elements of the Allied army too leniently, having released considerable numbers of prisoners. In August 1942 he was relieved of his command.

General Homma, born in 1888, was tried by the Allies for war crimes in September 1945 and executed by firing squad on 3 April 1946.

Japanese troops attacking in the Philippines. (author's collection)

Lieutenant-General Sir Brian Horrocks
British Army

The road to Arnhem. General Horrocks's XXX Corps became hopelessly bogged down on a narrow road, against tough enemy opposition. (author's collection)

Brian Horrocks was born on 7 September 1895 at the Indian hill station of Rannikat, the son of a distinguished officer of the Royal Army Medical Corps. He entered the Royal Military College, Sandhurst, in 1913, and was immediately sent to the front when war broke out with Germany the following year, but on 21 October 1914 he was wounded and taken prisoner, remaining in POW camps until the end of hostilities.

In 1919, Horrocks volunteered to serve with the British contingent of the Allied intervention force in Russia, supporting the loyalists in the Russian Civil War. With his unit, the 1st Battalion the Middlesex Regiment, he advanced from Vladivostok but was captured in some confused fighting, surviving both imprisonment and a bout of typhus to be repatriated in 1920. Horrocks – who was a notable athlete, representing his country in the pentathlon at the 1924 Olympic Games – made good progress in the peacetime army, and the outbreak of World War II found him in the post of senior instructor at the Staff College, Camberley.

In May 1940 he took command of the 2nd Battalion the Middlesex Regiment, just in time to lead it on its fighting retreat to Dunkirk. In June 1941 he was promoted acting major-general, and in March 1942 he was given command of the 9th Armoured Division, an extraordinary assignment for an infantry officer. On 14 August 1942, as a lieutenant-general, Horrocks was ordered to North Africa to take command of XIII Corps, which was part of General Montgomery's Eighth Army. Early in September, he conducted a superb defensive action at Alam Halfa, which was a serious setback for the Axis forces.

In December 1942 Horrocks was transferred to command X Corps, which was instrumental in breaking through the enemy positions in Tunisia in March 1943, but in June he was badly wounded in a strafing attack and sent back to England. It took him almost a year to recover, and he was still far from fit when he was ordered to France to command XXX Corps in August 1944, spearheading the drive across north-west Europe. In September, the Corps made a desperate attempt to reach the 1st British Airborne Division at Arnhem, but failed to arrive in time to prevent its destruction by the enemy.

Horrocks continued to lead XXX Corps in the final battles inside Germany, culminating in its capture of Bremen in May. He was invalided out of the Army in 1949, and subsequently led a varied life, becoming a noted writer, broadcaster and TV presenter. He died on 4 January 1985.

53

Admiral Miklos Horthy
Hungarian Statesman

Born in 1868, Miklos Horthy rose to the rank of admiral in the Austro-Hungarian Navy. In 1919 he was leader of the 'white terror' campaign against the short-lived communist regime of Bela Kun. After the departure of the Romanian forces of occupation, he became Regent of Hungary in March 1920. He was initially aggressively anti-Semitic, but this trait was gradually moderated. Throughout the 1920s and 1930s he conducted a conservative internal policy, and was a widely popular leader. The main objective of his foreign policy was the revision of the Treaty of Trianon (concluded in Versailles in 1920, when Hungary ceded about two-thirds of its pre-war territory), which brought him into growing co-operation with Nazi Germany. In February 1939 Hungary signed the Anti-Comintern Pact, and on 20 November 1940 also signed the German-Italian-Japanese Pact, thus definitely siding with the Axis powers. On 6 April 1941, Hungarian forces joined those of Germany and Italy in the invasion of Yugoslavia, and later played a not inconsiderable role in the fighting on the Russian Front.

Between 1938 and 1941, Horthy authorized a number of repressive anti-Jewish laws. However, in 1942 and 1943 he rejected German demands to impose even harsher measures, such as the exclusion of Jews from all economic activities and their deportation to ghettos and concentration camps. This attitude persisted only until the German occupation of Hungary in March 1944, when Horthy nominated a government that was totally subservient to the Nazis, giving it unlimited authority for anti-Jewish measures. Mass deportations followed, from which some 500,000 Jews never returned. Then, in August 1944, Horthy ordered the deportations to cease.

On 15 October 1944, following the lead of Romania, Horthy opened negotiations with the Russians with a view to concluding an armistice. This scheme was frustrated by German special forces under the command of the redoubtable SS Sturmbannführer Otto Skorzeny, who kidnapped Horthy and spirited him off to Germany. He was replaced by Ferenc Szalasi, the leader of the Fascist Arrow Cross Party.

Horthy was freed by the Allies in May 1945 and allowed to go to Portugal, where he died in 1946.

Miklos Horthy's scheme to surrender to the Russians was frustrated by German special forces, who staged a lightning coup. (Bundesarchiv)

Generaloberst Hermann Hoth
German Army

Hermann Hoth's Fourth Panzer Army attempted to break through to relieve the Sixth Army, trapped in Stalingrad, but proved too weak.
(Bundesarchiv)

One of the leading exponents of armoured warfare in the years between the two world wars, Hermann Hoth was born in Neuruppin, Germany, on 12 April 1885, the son of an army medical officer. He served in the army for the duration of World War 1, afterwards remaining in the Reichswehr, and in 1935, after Hitler's rise to power, he was given command of the 18th Division at Liegnitz. In November 1938, promoted to the rank of Generalleutnant, he took command of XV Motorized Corps, which he led in the Polish campaign and later in the attack on France, when XV Corps forced a passage of the river Meuse after infiltrating through the Ardennes. XV Corps, comprising two armoured divisions – one of which was commanded by a rising star called Erwin Rommel – subsequently made a dash for the Channel coast, which it reached in less than a week after crossing the Meuse. On 19 July, Hoth was promoted full general.

In the attack on Russia in June 1941 Hoth commanded Panzer Group 3, capturing Minsk and Vitebsk before racing on for Moscow. In October 1941, with the German offensive bogged down, Hoth was given command of Seventeenth Army in the Ukraine, which was subjected to heavy pressure by Soviet forces early in 1942. In June 1942, Hoth succeeded General Erich Hoepner as commander of Fourth Panzer Army, which was involved in the siege of Stalingrad; the plan envisaged Hoth's tanks breaking through to relieve the encircled Sixth Army, but in the face of mounting Soviet strength they proved too weak to achieve this goal. In July 1943 Hoth's forces were also committed to the unsuccessful attempt to break into the southern flank of the Kursk salient.

Hoth was recalled to Germany in November 1943 and spent the rest of the war on the reserve list. After the war, he was arrested and placed on trial at Nuremberg, charged with war crimes, and on 27 October 1948 he was sentenced to fifteen years in prison. Released after six years, he wrote several works on military history before his death in 1971.

Generaloberst Alfred Jodl
German Army

From 1942, Alfred Jodl was responsible for the conduct of all operations against the Western Allies. (Bundesarchiv)

Born on 10 May 1890, Alfred Jodl was a native of Würzburg. From 1903 to 1910 he attended the Bavarian Army Cadet School in Munich, after which he was commissioned into an artillery regiment. For the first two and a half years of World War I he served as a battery officer on the Western Front, being twice wounded. In 1917 he was attached to a Hungarian artillery regiment on the Eastern Front, and ended the war as an officer on the General Staff. After World War I he continued his service in the Reichswehr, and subsequently held various staff appointments, reaching the rank of Oberstleutnant in 1933. In 1939 he was appointed Chief of Staff to General Keitel, head of the Oberkommando der Wehrmacht, and in this capacity he became Hitler's closest adviser on the conduct of total war. He was promoted General in 1940. It was during this period that he made one of his greatest mistakes: he advised Hitler that, after the fall of France, Britain was in no position to fight on and would in all probability be compelled to sue for peace.

In 1942 Jodl took control of all operations against the Western Allies, which made him responsible for the conduct of the war from Norway to North Africa. A strong-willed and gifted strategist, he exerted far greater influence than his nominal superior, the ineffectual Keitel. In 1944 he was promoted Generaloberst, and in July that year was injured in the bomb plot against Hitler.

In May 1945, Jodl did his utmost to delay surrender negotiations with the Western Allies so that as many German troops as possible could break off combat with the Russians in the East and make their way westwards to surrender to the Americans and British, together with civilian refugees. The Allied Supreme Commander, General Eisenhower, realized what was happening and informed Jodl that, unless he ceased all pretence and delay, he would close the entire Allied front and prevent the escape from the East of any more Germans. The surrender document was duly signed by Jodl at Reims on 7 May.

In 1946, Generaloberst Alfred Jodl was found guilty of war crimes at Nuremberg, and was hanged on 16 October.

Generalfeldmarschall Wilhelm Keitel
German Army

Known by the derogatory nickname of Lakaitel (Little Lackey) because of his dog-like devotion to Hitler, Wilhelm Keitel was born in Helmscherode, near Braunschweig (Brunswick) on 22 September 1882. In 1901, after studying in Göttingen, he was commissioned into an artillery regiment; in 1902 he was promoted Leutnant, and in 1909 he was appointed regimental adjutant. During World War I, after serving on the General Staff, he held various field commands in Flanders, and was severely wounded. He was taken on by the Reichswehr in 1919, and in the 1920s, after service with an artillery regiment, he was assigned to the Reichswehrministerium, where he was responsible for frontier defence.

After the Nazi Party came to power in 1933 Keitel's advancement was rapid. In 1934 he was given command of a division in Bremen; in 1937 he was promoted to the rank of General, and in 1938 he was appointed Chief of Staff to the Oberkommando der Wehrmacht, a newly created administrative body which directly subordinated all the German armed forces to the authority of Adolf Hitler. In this capacity he executed Hitler's commands to the letter, no matter how abhorrent they were, and constantly acted as a buffer between the Führer and the German generals, most of whom voiced their disapproval of Hitler's decisions at some point.

Keitel played a major part in the administration of those areas of the Soviet Union occupied by the Germans after their invasion of June 1941, resulting in the harshest punishments being meted out to Russian civilians. He also directed the use of Russian prisoners of war as forced labourers.

On 8 May 1945, Keitel, as the emissary of Admiral Doenitz, signed the unconditional surrender of all German forces in the presence of the Soviet generals who had conducted the battle for Berlin. On 13 May he surrendered himself to the British, and was subsequently indicted for war crimes. He was found guilty at Nuremberg, and sentenced to death by hanging. The execution was carried out on 16 October 1946.

To his dying day, Generalfeldmarschall Wilhelm Keitel remained slavishly devoted to Adolf Hitler and the Nazi cause. (Bundesarchiv)

Generalfeldmarschall Albert Kesselring
German Army

'Smiling Albert' Kesselring, as he was nicknamed by his troops, inherited a host of problems when he was appointed C-in-C South. (via Philip Jarrett)

Born at Bayreuth, Germany, on 8 August 1885, the son of a schoolteacher, Albert Kesselring joined the German Army in 1904 as a subaltern with the 2nd Bavarian Foot Artillery Regiment at Mainz. In World War I he served as a brigade adjutant and general staff officer, remaining in the Army after the end of hostilities. In 1933, Hermann Goering, with whom he had become friendly during the war, persuaded him to transfer to the newly formed (and still secret) Luftwaffe, where he became head of the Administration Office. In 1934 he was promoted to general rank, and in mid-1936 was appointed to the post of Luftwaffe Chief of Staff. In 1938 he assumed command of Luftwaffengruppe 1, a post which he retained until shortly before the German invasion of Poland in 1939, when he was given command of Luftflotte 1. Early in 1940 he assumed command of Luftflotte 2, whose operations he conducted through the Battles of France and Britain, and the early stages of the campaign in Russia from June 1941. He remained in command when, in December 1941, Luftflotte 2 moved to the Mediterranean theatre, and shortly afterwards he was placed in overall command of all German forces in the area with the title of Commander-in-Chief South.

Kesselring proved himself to be an able and talented commander, but he had to contend with some serious problems which, ultimately, proved insurmountable. First there was the island of Malta, the strategic key to the central Mediterranean, which remained unbroken under a fierce Axis air onslaught and whose strike aircraft and submarines took a fearsome toll of Axis shipping; then there was the question of relationships between the Germans and their Italian allies, which became increasingly strained as the war in North Africa went on and which needed careful manipulation. Another key problem was the impetuosity of Erwin Rommel, who, after defeating the British decisively at Gazala in June 1942, plunged on towards the prize of the Suez Canal despite being starved of supplies and equipment, and who was himself decisively defeated at El Alamein in November.

After the expulsion of the Axis forces from North Africa in May 1943, Kesselring remained as C-in-C South in command of the German forces in Italy, where his expert defensive strategy prevented the Allies from achieving a decisive breakthrough. In March 1945 he was appointed C-in-C West, an appointment he held for a few weeks before Germany's final surrender. Tried as a war criminal, Kesselring was sentenced to death by a British military tribunal in 1947, but was pardoned and released in 1952. He died in 1960, after having spent some years as president of Stahlhelm, the German War Veterans' Association.

Fleet Admiral Ernest J. King
US Navy

Ernest Joseph King, the man one day destined to command the largest fleet the world had ever seen, was born into a strict Calvinist family in Lorain, Ohio, on 23 November 1878. He graduated from the US Naval Academy in 1901 and subsequently served on a variety of warships, large and small. By the end of World War I he had risen to the rank of captain, and in the 1920s he commanded a submarine flotilla and the submarine base at New London, Connecticut. In 1928, following flight training and further sea service, King was appointed Assistant Chief of the Bureau of Aeronautics. In 1930 he was given command of the aircraft-carrier USS *Lexington*, and in 1933, now a rear-admiral, he was made Chief of the Bureau of Aeronautics.

During the late 1930s King commanded the US Battle Fleet's aircraft-carrier force, and early in 1941 he was appointed to command the newly formed Atlantic Fleet. In December 1941, following the Japanese attack on Pearl Harbor, he was appointed Commander-in-Chief of the US Fleet, and in the following year he was made Chief of Naval Operations. His greatest achievements were to inspire and oversee major innovations in carrier-based air tactics, and in conducting amphibious landings, notably at Guadalcanal in 1942, which gave the Americans a base for their future conduct of the Pacific war.

King never made any secret of the fact that he did not like the British, an outlook that stemmed from his service in the Atlantic during World War I, and he consistently advocated that the resources of the United States should be directed towards defeating Japan first. Fortunately, he was just as consistently overruled by President Roosevelt. However, he was shrewd enough to realize that the Allies had to work in close concert, and never was this more apparent than when he provided extra naval forces for the D-Day landings in Normandy at the request of the British Admiralty, many British warships being tied to convoy escort duty in the Atlantic.

In December 1944 King was promoted Fleet Admiral. He retired in the following year and died on 25 June 1956, after a long period of ill-health.

Prickly and difficult to work with, Fleet Admiral King was nevertheless a talented organizer. (National Archives)

General Philippe Leclerc
French Army

Philippe Leclerc was actually born at Belloy-St-Léonard in 1902 under the name of Philippe François Marie de Hauteclocque, assuming the name Leclerc at a later date. In 1940, he was the first to answer General de Gaulle's appeal of 18 June 1940 that France should continue fighting. Arrested by the Vichy government, which he totally opposed, Leclerc escaped twice, and was sent by de Gaulle to French Equatorial Africa, where he raised a Free French force some 2,500 strong and led it north from Lake Chad across the Sahara for 1,500 miles to join the British Commonwealth forces fighting in the Western Desert after the Battle of Alamein. Leclerc placed his force unreservedly under the command of General Montgomery, and his troops made a valuable contribution to the Tunisian campaign of 1943. Montgomery's Chief of Staff, Major-General Sir Francis de Guingand, later recalled Leclerc's arrival: 'At first I thought one of the characters of Wren's "Beau Geste" had come along to pay a call. His appearance personified the hardened French colonial soldier. He was thin and drawn, but instantly alert. His clothes had long since seen their day. Thin drill uniform with threadbare breeches, and old but shapely riding boots. A French képi completed the picture.'

In 1944, Leclerc assumed command of the 2nd French Armoured Division, and on 1 August 1944 his forces landed in Normandy, attached to the US Third Army, in time to take part in the breakout and subsequent advance to the river Seine. His crowning glory came on 24 August, when the tanks of his division moved in to liberate Paris and Leclerc accepted the surrender of the German commander, General von Choltitz. Leclerc's forces subsequently drove on to assist in the capture of Strasbourg in conjunction with the US VI Corps, breaking through the enemy defences to reach the Rhine. Its final operation, in April 1945, was to join with US forces in the capture of Berchtesgaden, Hitler's mountain retreat in the Bavarian Alps.

With the war in Europe over, General Leclerc was sent to the Far East to represent France at the final surrender of Japan in September 1945. In 1952, he was killed in an air crash in North Africa, and received a posthumous promotion to Marshal of France.

Tanks of General Leclerc's 2nd Armoured Division roll into Paris, August 1944. (author's collection)

Air Chief Marshal Sir Trafford Leigh-Mallory
Royal Air Force

Although never outstanding as a fighter commander, Trafford Leigh-Mallory was a leading exponent of air–ground co-operation. (IWM)

The man who was to be at the centre of a major argument between the RAF commanders in the Battle of Britain was born at Mobberley, Cheshire, on 17 November 1892. He graduated with honours in history from Cambridge University, and on the outbreak of World War I he joined the territorial battalion of the King's Regiment, later being commissioned into the Lancashire Fusiliers. He was wounded at Ypres in 1915, and in July 1916, on his recovery, he transferred to the Royal Flying Corps. By April 1918 he was a major in command of No. 8 Squadron, flying Armstrong Whitworth FK.8 army co-operation aircraft as part of the Fifteenth Corps Wing, and during his active service he was awarded the DSO and DFC.

During the inter-war years Leigh-Mallory amassed a great deal of experience in air–ground co-operation. In 1931 he became Deputy Director of Staff Studies at the Air Ministry, and a tour as officer commanding No. 2 Flying Training School was followed by a staff post in Iraq. In 1937, promoted to the rank of air vice-marshal, he was appointed to command No. 12 Fighter Group, and he was still in this post on the outbreak of World War II. During the Battle of Britain he came into conflict with Air Chief Marshal Sir High Dowding, AOC-in-C Fighter Command,

and Air Vice-Marshal Keith Park, commanding No. 11 Group in the forefront of the battle, over a number of issues, not the least of which was the 'big wing' concept. This involved large numbers of fighters being assembled to attack the enemy, rather than attacks being made by individual squadrons; Park justifiably argued that his fighter bases were too close to the front line – in other words, the English Channel – to permit the assembly of large defensive formations once the alarm sounded.

Ironically, it was Leigh-Mallory who succeeded Park when the latter was relieved as commander of No. 11 Group in November 1940. In November 1942, Leigh-Mallory became Air Officer Commanding-in-Chief, RAF Fighter Command. He received a knighthood in January 1943, and later that year was appointed commander of the Allied Expeditionary Air Forces that were being assembled to lend tactical support for the coming invasion of Europe. With the invasion successfully completed, he was appointed to command the Allied Air Forces in South-East Asia, but it was an appointment he was destined never to keep. On 14 November 1944, he and his wife were killed when the Avro York transport that was taking them to the Far East crashed in the mountains near Grenoble.

General Curtis E. LeMay
US Army Air Force

Ruthless and efficient, Curtis LeMay directed the USAAF's massive bomber offensive against Japan in the closing months of WWII. (USAF)

Curtis Emerson LeMay was born at Columbus, Ohio, on 15 November 1906 and graduated from Ohio State University. In 1928 he entered the US Army Air Corps as a flight cadet, completing his flying training in the following year. His first tour of duty was with the 27th Pursuit Squadron at Selfridge Field, Michigan, and he completed several tours with fighter units before transferring to bombers in 1937. He subsequently took part in a number of long-range bomber exercises, including the first mass deployment of 2nd Bomb Group B-17s to South America in 1938. Prior to America's entry into World War II, LeMay pioneered air routes over the South Atlantic to Africa and over the North Atlantic to England.

In 1942, LeMay organized and trained the 305th Bomb Group, which deployed to Bovingdon, England, in September 1942, and led it on operations, developing the formation procedures and bombing techniques that would be used by B-17 units throughout the European theatre. In August 1943, as Commanding General of the Third Bomb Division, he led the famous (and costly) attack on Regensburg, the B-17s leaving their English bases and flying on to airfields in North Africa. In July 1944 LeMay was transferred to the Pacific theatre to direct strategic bombing operations, first of all by B-29s of the 20th Bomber Command in the China–Burma–India theatre, and then by 21st Bomber Command from bases in the Pacific, from where the heavy bombers were able to strike at Japan in strength. In the closing stages of the Pacific war he became Chief of Staff of the Strategic Air Forces in the Pacific, and at the end of hostilities he piloted a B-29 on a non-stop, record-breaking flight from Hokkaido, Japan, to Chicago, Illinois.

General LeMay subsequently served in the Pentagon as the first Deputy Chief of Air Staff for Research and Development, before going to Wiesbaden, Germany, in October 1947 to assume command of the United States Air Forces in Europe (USAFE). His tour of duty there encompassed the dangerous period of the Berlin Airlift. On 16 October 1948 he took command of the newly formed Strategic Air Command (SAC), a post he was to hold for nearly a decade. In July 1957 General LeMay was appointed USAF Vice-Chief of Staff, and on 30 July 1961 Chief of Staff. He retired on 31 July 1965, having witnessed SAC grow into the most formidable fighting force the world had ever seen.

General LeMay remained active in defence affairs and also entered third-party politics, being selected as presidential candidate of the American Independent Party and enjoying considerable success. He died on 3 October 1990.

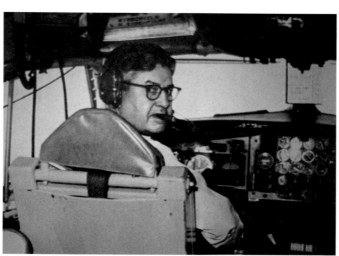

General LeMay seen at the controls of a Boeing KC-135 Stratotanker when he was Commanding General, Strategic Air Command. (USAF)

Admiral Gunther Lütjens
German Navy

The son of a merchant, Gunther Lütjens was born in Wiesbaden, Germany, on 25 May 1889. He entered naval college in 1907, and during World War I he commanded flotillas of gunboats and torpedo-boats, and took part in some successful actions off the Belgian coast. On one occasion, on 2 May 1917, he led four torpedo-boats against four British coastal motor-boats (CMBs) off Ostende, sinking two of the latter and heavily damaging the others.

Lütjens left the Navy at the end of World War I and worked for a time as an official at the Warnemunde Shipping Agency before returning to service in 1923. During the inter-war years he maintained his association with coastal craft, commanding the 3rd Torpedo-Boat Flotilla. In 1936, as a member of the new Kriegsmarine, he was appointed head of personnel, and then moved to a new post as Commander, Destroyers and Torpedo-Boats. During the Norwegian campaign of April and May 1940, as a Vizeadmiral, he commanded the covering force for the German landings in northern Norway, comprising the battlecruisers *Scharnhorst* and *Gneisenau*. In the winter of 1940–41 he took the same two warships out into the Atlantic on a commerce-raiding spree that cost the Allies 22 merchant ships totalling 115,622 tons.

This success encouraged the Germans to launch a much bigger operation, involving a battle group comprising the new battleship *Bismarck*, the heavy cruiser *Prinz Eugen* and the two battlecruisers, with Lütjens as fleet commander. In the event, the *Scharnhorst* and *Gneisenau* remained penned up in the French Atlantic port of Brest, *Gneisenau* having been badly damaged in a torpedo attack by an RAF aircraft, and only the *Bismarck* and *Prinz Eugen* set sail in May 1941, breaking out into the North Atlantic. Intercepted by British naval forces, on 24

A fine officer, Lütjens believed in the welfare of his men, but sacrificed them by ordering Bismarck's *crew to fight to the end. (author's collection)*

May there was an exchange of gunfire in which the British battlecruiser HMS *Hood* was sunk and the battleship *Prince of Wales* damaged, but two days later, the German warships having parted company, *Bismarck* was attacked by Fairey Swordfish torpedo-bombers, which damaged her rudders and made her unmanageable. Shelled to pieces by British battleships and torpedoed by cruisers, she sank on 27 May with the loss of some 2,100 men and the entire fleet staff, including Admiral Lütjens.

Bismarck *and* Prinz Eugen *were to have teamed up with* Gneisenau *and* Scharnhorst, *whose crew is seen here being inspected by Vizeadmiral Ciliax. (author's collection)*

General Douglas MacArthur
US Army

Douglas MacArthur was born into a military family (his father was General Arthur MacArthur, who was Governor of the Philippines) in 1880, and subsequently attended the US Military Academy at West Point, graduating top of his class in 1903. He then served in the Philippines and in Japan before becoming aide to President Theodore Roosevelt in 1906–7. From 1913 to 1917 he was attached to the US Army General Staff. As commander of the US 42nd Division in World War I, he was outstandingly successful during the Second Battle of the Marne in 1918. He was superintendent of West Point from 1919 to 1922, and Army Chief of Staff from 1930 to 1935, during which period he spent two years in the Philippines, preparing the islands for independence.

MacArthur retired from the Army in 1937, but was recalled to active duty in July 1941, when it seemed that war with Japan was likely. He was appointed commander of the US and Filipino forces in the Philippines, and did his utmost to create strong defences, specially in terms of aircraft; but Allied air power in the islands was still woefully inadequate when the Japanese attacked Pearl Harbor. When numerically superior Japanese forces, with strong air support, thrust into the Philippines, MacArthur executed a professional fighting retreat, slowing down the enemy advance to such an extent that the islands were not fully occupied until May 1942. Two months before this, President Roosevelt

had ordered MacArthur to safety. As he departed, he vowed to return.

MacArthur's primary task as Commander-in-Chief, South-West Pacific, was to turn Australia into a huge military base in preparation for a series of offensives that would drive the Japanese back to their home islands. It was from Australia that MacArthur launched the New Guinea campaign, which was crucial to the reconquest of the Pacific, and later, in 1944, the campaign that resulted in the retaking of the Philippines. On 2 September 1945, MacArthur accepted the Japanese surrender on behalf of the Allies on board the battleship USS *Missouri* in Tokyo Bay. He was then appointed commander of the Allied Forces of Occupation in Japan, a position of unlimited power which he exercised firmly but wisely.

In 1950, when North Korean forces invaded the south, MacArthur was placed in command of the United Nations military response, and within a few months he had thrown the North Koreans back and invaded their country. When the Chinese entered the conflict, MacArthur's proposal to extend the war to China, and perhaps use nuclear weapons, led to his dismissal by President Truman. He retired as a five-star general and faded from public view, living quietly in New York until his death in 1964. It may be said, with justification, that Douglas MacArthur was one of the finest strategists in the history of warfare.

General Douglas MacArthur vowed to return to the Philippines, and was as good as his word. (National Archives)

Marshal Rodion Y. Malinovsky
Soviet Army

Rodion Malinovsky directed Russia's successful but costly offensives on the Southern Front. (via J. R. Cavanagh)

Born in the Ukraine in 1898, Rodion Yakovlevich Malinovsky served in the Imperial Russian Army during World War I, transferring his allegiance to the Red Army in 1919 and joining the Communist Party in 1926. In 1930 he graduated from the Frunze Military Academy, subsequently serving as Chief of Staff of a cavalry regiment, in the headquarters of various military districts, and as Chief of Staff of a cavalry corps. From 1936 to 1939 he was one of the principal Soviet advisers to the Republican government during the Spanish Civil War, afterwards returning to the Frunze Academy as an instructor.

At the time of Germany's invasion of the Soviet Union in June 1941 Malinovsky was in command of a rifle corps. In 1942 he was made Deputy Commander of the Voronezh Front, and later in the year he commanded the 2nd Guards Army during the Battle of Stalingrad. During 1943 he successively commanded the Southern, South-Western, 3rd and 2nd Ukrainian Fronts. In the summer of 1943, it was Malinovksy's South-Western Front that followed-up the Soviet victories at Kursk and Orel by pushing across the Donets to join up with the Southern Front in a bid to envelop the German Army Group South.

In 1944 Rodion Malinovsky was made a Marshal of the Soviet Union, and in August that year his 2nd Ukrainian Front joined with the 3rd Ukrainian to begin a powerful new offensive which, after five days, completely surrounded the German Army Group South Ukraine. The total losses suffered by this Army Group exceeded half a million men. Between 20 August and 3 September alone the Soviet forces took 208,000 prisoners, including 21 generals. By the end of September, Malinovsky's forces had swept across Romania to the borders of Hungary and Yugoslavia, and subsequently pressed on to encircle 188,000 enemy troops in Budapest, finally bringing about their destruction in February 1945.

With the European war at an end, Malinovsky was placed in command of the Transbaikal Front, which was engaged in the brief campaign against the Japanese in Manchuria in August 1945. In 1947, he was appointed Commander-in-Chief of the Soviet forces in the Far East and subsequently held a number of very senior military posts, becoming Minister of Defence in 1957. He held this post until his death ten years later.

Generalfeldmarschall Erich von Manstein
German Army

Released from prison in 1953, Erich von Manstein played a leading part in the formation of the new Federal German Army. (Bundesarchiv)

Erich von Manstein was actually born in Berlin on 24 November 1887 as Fritz-Erich von Lewinski, the son of Artillery General Eduard von Lewinski. When his father was killed on a military exercise, the boy was adopted by Georg von Manstein, and took the latter's name. In 1906 Manstein joined the 3rd Guards Infantry Regiment, being commissioned as Leutnant in 1907. He saw action during World War I, notably at Verdun and on the Somme, and also attended the Prussian Military Academy. By the end of the conflict he was a Hauptmann, and a divisional staff officer. He remained in the Reichswehr after the war, being promoted Major in 1927 and serving in various administrative commands. In 1936, now an Oberst, he was appointed adjutant to General Ludwig Beck, Chief of Staff of the newly formed Wehrmacht, and in 1937 he was made Deputy Chief of the General Staff, a post accompanied by promotion to Generalmajor.

In October 1939, following the campaign in Poland, Manstein, now a Generalleutnant and Chief of Staff of Army Group A, formulated a plan for an attack on the Low Countries and France. His idea was to launch the main axis of the attack through the supposedly impassable Ardennes, and this was implemented with huge success in May 1940, leading to the collapse of France within seven weeks and the evacuation of the British Expeditionary Force from Dunkirk. In July, following the successful conclusion of the campaign in the west, Manstein was made a full General and awarded the Ritterkreuz. In November, he took command of LVI Panzerkorps in East Prussia.

In June 1941, at the start of the German invasion of Russia, Manstein's armour advanced through the Baltic States towards Leningrad. In September, he was appointed commander-in-chief of the most southerly sector of the Eastern Front, and in 1942 his 11th Army overcame stiff Russian resistance to overrun the Crimea and capture the fortress of Sevastopol. Perhaps his greatest achievement, however, was in stabilizing the front after the German Sixth Army was encircled and destroyed at Stalingrad in 1943, recapturing Kharkov in a brilliantly executed flanking movement.

In March 1944, following serious differences with Adolf Hitler over the conduct of the war in the east, Manstein was relieved of his command. Captured by the British in May 1945, he went before a British military tribunal in October 1949 and was sentenced to twelve years' imprisonment for war crimes, but was released in May 1953 and became official adviser to the Federal German government on the construction of the new Bundeswehr. He died on 11 June 1973, at Irschenhausen, Bavaria. Arguably the best battlefield commander of the European war, he wrote his memoirs, entitled *Verlorene Siege* ('Lost Victories').

General George C. Marshall
US Army

A rare combination of soldier and statesman, General George Catlett Marshall's career ran closely parallel to the first half of the twentieth century. Born in Uniontown, Pennsylvania, on 31 December 1880, he graduated from the Virginia Military Institute in 1902 and was commissioned into the infantry in 1902. He served in the Philippines from 1902 to 1903, and in 1907 he came top of his class at the School of the Line, Fort Leavenworth, Kansas. After completing a more advanced course, he remained at Leavenworth as an instructor from 1908 to 1910. From 1913 to 1916 he served a second tour in the Philippines, and in 1917 he went with the US 1st Infantry Division to France, where as chief of operations he was heavily involved in campaign planning work. Later, assigned to GHQ, he helped plan the US attack in the St-Mihiel salient and the Meuse-Argonne offensive, serving as Chief of Operations, US First Army, in the final weeks of the war.

From 1919 to 1924 Marshall was senior aide to General John J. Pershing, the US Army commander, and from 1924 to 1927 he was executive officer of the 15th Infantry Regiment at Tientsin, China. Returning to the US, he rose to be a brigade commander in 1936, and in 1939, on the nomination of President Franklin D. Roosevelt, he became Chief of Staff of the American Army, a post in which he served until November 1945. During this period he increased the strength of the army from 200,000 in 1939 to almost 8.5 million in 1945. He was present at all the great conferences of the war, from Argentia, Newfoundland, in 1941 to Potsdam in the summer of 1945. He was firmly in favour of the strategy that involved a cross-Channel invasion in 1944, and put an enormous amount of effort into planning the same. The British Prime Minister, Winston Churchill, called him the 'true organizer of victory'.

Marshall's two greatest achievements were to support Churchill in advocating the defeat of Germany before Japan, and his post-war European Recovery Program (generally known as the Marshall Plan) in which huge sums of dollars were invested in bankrupt Europe to speed its economic recovery and form a bulwark against Soviet expansion. In 1950, as head of the US Department of Defense, he helped develop the North Atlantic Treaty Organization (NATO). In December 1953 he was awarded the Nobel Peace Prize, the only professional soldier ever to receive this honour.

General Marshall died on 16 October 1959.

General George C. Marshall was a firm advocate of the policy of defeating Germany first, then turning on Japan. (National Archives)

Major-General Frank D. Merrill
US Army

Frank Dow Merrill was born at Hopkinton, Massachusetts, on 4 December 1903. He joined the US Army in 1922 and graduated from the Military Academy, West Point, in 1928. He obtained a BSc degree in engineering from the Massachusetts Institute of Technology. In 1938 he was assigned to the US Embassy in Tokyo as Assistant Military Attaché, and took the opportunity to learn Japanese and Chinese during his tour there. At the beginning of 1941 he was promoted temporary major and assigned to Manila, in the Philippines, as General Douglas MacArthur's intelligence officer.

At the time of the Japanese attack on Pearl Harbor in December 1941 Merrill was in Rangoon, Burma, on a mission for MacArthur, and was assigned to the China–Burma–India theatre of operations. In the spring of 1942 he was promoted to lieutenant-colonel and subsequently took part in a number of actions against the Japanese, being wounded. In October 1943 Merrill was appointed operations officer for the CBI theatre under General Joseph

Stilwell, and as such he organized the 5307th Composite Unit (Provisional), a long-range penetration group whose task was to operate deep inside enemy territory, in much the same way as the British Chindits. After intensive training in jungle warfare, the group, which became known as 'Merrill's Marauders', went into action in February 1944, harassing Japanese lines of communication in Burma. In May 1944, reinforced by Chinese troops, they captured the key airfield at Myitkyina; the town itself fell three months later.

After serving as deputy commander of US forces in the CBI, Merrill, now a major-general, was appointed Chief of Staff of the US 10th Army in Okinawa, and in 1947 he headed a military advisory group to the Republic of the Philippines, which was seeking to stabilize itself after the years of Japanese occupation. He retired in 1948 and became New Hampshire's Highway Commissioner, but the years in Burma had taken their toll, and in 1955, aged only 52, he died of a heart attack while attending a convention at Fernandina Beach, Florida.

Frank D. Merrill as a West Point cadet in the 1920s.
(National Archives)

Marshal Giovanni Messe
Italian Army

Allied forces storming ashore in North Africa, November 1944. Six months later, the Axis forces there were defeated.
(National Archives)

Undoubtedly one of Italy's best senior officers of World War II, Giovanni Messe was born near Brindisi on 10 December 1883. He saw action in World War I, and subsequently took part in counter-insurgency operations in the Italian colonies and in the expedition against Abyssinia (Ethiopia) in the 1930s. In 1939 he was appointed deputy commander of the Italian forces of occupation in Albania, and in 1941 he commanded an army corps during the Greek campaign. In 1941, he was appointed commander of the Corpo de Spedizione Italiano (CSIR), the Italian Expeditionary Force that fought alongside the Germans and Romanians on the Eastern Front, and in March 1943, when General Erwin Rommel was promoted to commander of Heeresgruppe Afrika, Messe was given command of Panzerarmee Afrika, now renamed the First Italian Army. His arrival coincided with a monumental wrangle that was going on between the Italians and Germans over questions of policy. Messe openly expressed his dislike at being given such a command at such a time, for by now the Axis forces were

hemmed into Tunisia and were under fierce pressure on all sides. In the event his protest was of a purely academic nature, for the Germans still exercised their authority over the First Italian Army through its German Chief of Staff, General Fritz Bayerlein. With the war in North Africa lost, however, it was Messe who had to make the final crucial decisions, and he had only one option left open to him. On 12 May 1943, he was promoted marshal, and the next day he surrendered to the British. He conducted these proceedings in an extremely dignified manner, which was in sharp contrast to the churlish attitude displayed by the man who had taken over from Rommel as commander of Heeresgruppe Afrika, Generaloberst Jürgen von Arnim.

After Italy's armistice with the Allies in September 1943 Messe served as Chief of Staff to the Co-Belligerent Italian Army, a post he retained until 1945. From 1953 to 1955 he was elected to the Italian parliament, but then retired and devoted his life to writing his memoirs. He died on 19 December, 1968.

Generalfeldmarschall Walther Model
German Army

In the second half of 1944 Generalfeldmarschall Model, seen here on the left, conducted an expert fighting retreat through north-west Europe. (Bundesarchiv)

Born on 24 January 1891, at Genthin, near Magdeburg, Walther Model entered the Imperial German Army in 1909 and served with distinction during World War I, being decorated for bravery at the Battle of Verdun. He served in the post-war Reichswehr, and after Hitler came to power in 1933 he dedicated himself to the Nazi cause. By 1938 he had risen to the rank of Generalmajor, and commanded the 4th Army during the German invasion of Poland in 1939. He was Chief of Staff of the 16th Army during the Campaign in the West, May–June 1940, and in July he received promotion to Generalleutnant in recognition of his services.

During the invasion of the Soviet Union in June 1941, Model commanded the 3rd Panzer Division. A forceful and energetic field commander, he earned the nickname 'The Führer's Fireman', because Hitler repeatedly ordered him to take command in places where the Germans were under serious pressure. Promoted to full General in 1942, Model was placed in command of the 9th Army, and in 1943 he was involved in the planning of Operation Citadel, which developed into the massive armoured confrontation at Kursk in August. In January 1944 Model took command of Army Group North, and successively commanded Army Group North

Ukraine (March 1944) and Army Group Centre (June 1944). It was while he was in command of Army Group Centre that he recorded his most notable achievement – halting the Soviet offensive near Warsaw.

Model, a Generalfeldmarschall since March 1944, was given command of the German forces on the Western Front in August, as the Allies began the breakout from Normandy. He was unable to stop the Allied advance through north-west Europe, although he expertly rallied the retreating German forces and organized a series of temporary defensive lines based on natural barriers, such as rivers, that stopped the retreat from becoming a rout. When command of the German forces in the West was assumed by Generalfeldmarschall Rundstedt in September 1944, Model took command of Army Group B, concentrated in Holland, where his forces prevented the British 1st Airborne Division from seizing the bridge over the Rhine at Arnhem. Model was largely instrumental in planning and executing the Ardennes offensive of December 1944, but this was a final gamble, and when it was contained the remnants of Army Group B were encircled in the Ruhr. Model ordered the Army Group, still comprising some 300,000 men, to disband, and on 21 April 1945 he shot himself.

Field Marshal Viscount Montgomery of Alamein British Army

Of Ulster stock, the son of a bishop, Bernard Law Montgomery was born in London on 17 November 1887, and attended St Paul's School in the city. In 1908 he graduated from the Royal Military Academy, Sandhurst, and was commissioned into the Royal Warwickshire Regiment as a 2nd lieutenant. He served with distinction on the Western Front during World War I, winning the DSO. In 1931 he commanded the 1st Battalion and afterwards rose rapidly in rank, commanding the 8th Infantry Division in Palestine and Transjordan as a major-general in 1938–9, during the Arab Rebellion. At the outbreak of World War II he went to France in command of the 3rd Infantry Division. Having evacuated his men from Dunkirk in May 1940, he was given command of V Corps in Britain, then XII Corps, until, in 1942, he became C-in-C South-East Command.

On 18 August 1942, Montgomery assumed command of the Eighth Army in Egypt, then under heavy pressure from Rommel's Axis forces, and in the ensuing months he displayed the brilliant leadership that firmly established his reputation as one of the greatest generals of the war. After meticulous preparation (a Montgomery hallmark), he launched an attack on the Axis forces entrenched at El Alamein in northern Egypt on 23 October, and when their lines broke he pursued them into Libya and beyond, thus becoming the first of the Allied generals to inflict a decisive defeat upon the enemy. On 10 November he was knighted and promoted to full general.

Still leading the Eighth Army, Montgomery participated in the Allied landing on Sicily in July 1943 and led the troops invading the Italian mainland two months later. In January 1944 he returned to Britain to command all land forces under General Eisenhower preparing for the invasion of Europe. After the Allied landing in Normandy in June 1944, Montgomery directed all land operations until August, when the command was reorganized. He was then made commander of 21st Army Group, comprising the Canadian 1st and British 2nd Armies, which held the northern end of the Allied line. In September 1944 he suffered his worst setback of the war with the loss of the 1st British Airborne Division at Arnhem.

On 17 December 1944, after the German offensive in the Ardennes had split the Allied 12th Army Group, Montgomery was given temporary command of all British and American forces on the northern side of the 'bulge'. The offensive was halted and thrown back, and the Allies pushed on into Germany, where, on 4 May 1945, Montgomery accepted the surrender of all German forces in the Netherlands and north-west Germany. On 22 May, he was appointed head of the British Forces of Occupation and a member of the Allied Control Commission.

Raised to the peerage as the 1st Viscount Montgomery of Alamein in 1946, he was made Chief of the Imperial General Staff. From 1948 to 1951 he served as chairman of the permanent defence organization of the Western European Union, and he was Deputy Supreme Commander of NATO from 1951 until his retirement in 1958.

Viscount Montgomery, KG, GCB, DSO, died at Alton, Hampshire, on 24 March 1976.

One of the most controversial commanders of World War II, Montgomery would never launch an offensive unless he enjoyed overwhelming superiority.

Earl Mountbatten of Burma
Royal Navy

A great-grandson of Queen Victoria, and the son of Prince Louis of Battenberg, who became First Sea Lord in 1912, Louis Mountbatten was born in Windsor, England, on 25 June 1900. His original name was Louis Francis Albert Victor Nicholas of Battenberg; it was later changed because of its Germanic origins. In 1914 Mountbatten entered the Royal Naval College, Dartmouth, and was commissioned as a midshipman in 1916, serving on the battlecruiser HMS *Lion* and then in *P.31*, an anti-submarine patrol vessel. In 1934 he gained his first command, the destroyer HMS *Daring*, and by mid-1939 he was in command of a flotilla of destroyers.

Captain Lord Mountbatten was in the thick of the fighting almost from the beginning of World War II. His destroyer, HMS *Kelly*, which led the 5th Destroyer Flotilla, was seriously damaged off Norway in April 1940 and had to be towed to port. In April 1941 the flotilla was transferred to the Mediterranean theatre, just in time to see action during the German invasion of Crete, and on 23 May *Kelly* was sunk by German dive-bombers, together with a sister ship, *Kashmir*.

In October 1941, while waiting for another seagoing command, Mountbatten was appointed Director of Combined Operations, in which capacity he organized exploratory commando raids on France and Norway, notably the disastrous raid on Dieppe in August 1942, which resulted in massive casualties among the Canadian troops involved.

In August 1943, Admiral Lord Louis Mountbatten was appointed Supreme Allied Commander, South-East Asia. Although he experienced some early difficulties, not the least of which was the Admiralty's failure to define his responsibilities clearly, he went on to achieve an excellent degree of co-operation between British, Empire, American and Chinese forces under his command, using a mixture of innate charm and tactful firmness. Under his jurisdiction, the Allies halted the Japanese advance into India at the decisive battles of Imphal and Kohima, and then launched the reconquest of Burma.

After Japan's surrender, Mountbatten had the tricky task of repatriating Allied and Japanese personnel to their various homelands and of negotiating with the rash of post-colonial governments that were emerging throughout South-East Asia. In March 1947 he became Viceroy of India, the last person to hold this post, and remained as interim Governor-General until June 1948, overseeing the difficult and sometimes bloody partition between India and Pakistan.

In October 1948 Mountbatten returned to the Mediterranean Station as rear-admiral in command of the 1st Cruiser Squadron, and from 1952 to 1954 he was Commander-in-Chief, Allied Forces Mediterranean. This was followed by appointments as First Sea Lord (1955–9) and Chief of the Defence Staff (1959–65).

Earl Mountbatten was murdered by the IRA (Irish Republican Army) in 1979, when a bomb exploded in the yacht in which he was sailing off the Irish coast.

As the Supreme Allied Commander in South-East Asia, Lord Mountbatten had one of the most difficult tasks of any wartime leader. (National Archives)

Benito Mussolini
Italian Fascist Dictator

Benito Mussolini in typically heroic posture. (via J. R. Cavanagh)

Mussolini felt strong enough to order a march on Rome, where King Victor Emmanuel III appointed him Prime Minister. In 1928 he ended parliamentary government and established himself as dictator, with the title of Duce (Leader). In 1929 he concluded the Lateran Treaty with the Papacy, bringing to an end a conflict between Church and State, and inaugurated a massive building programme, his aim being to restore Italy to the grandeur of Roman times.

In October 1935, after several months of military preparation, Italian forces invaded Abyssinia, an act that isolated Mussolini from the international community with the exception of Germany, with whose leader, Adolf Hitler, he began to form a closer relationship. During the Spanish Civil War, both Germany and Italy sent expeditionary forces to the aid of the Nationalists. In 1938, Mussolini made no protest when Hitler annexed Austria, and in the following year his own forces invaded Albania.

In June 1940, with France on the verge of collapse and the defeat of Britain seeming certain, Mussolini entered the war on the side of Germany, but the myth of his invincibility was soon shattered: first in North Africa, when British and Dominion forces inflicted shattering defeats on his armies, and then in Greece, where his offensive from Albania was halted and then driven back. In both areas, the Germans had to intervene to rescue the situation.

In July 1943, with the Axis forces in North Africa defeated and Sicily invaded, Mussolini's personal prestige collapsed and the Fascist Grand Council was no longer prepared to tolerate his leadership. He was dismissed by the King, who then ordered his arrest, and he was incarcerated in an hotel in the Abruzzi mountains. In September 1943, however, he was rescued by German airborne forces led by SS Sturmbannführer Otto Skorzeny. Adolf Hitler installed him as head of a puppet government in northern Italy, but when Germany collapsed in April 1945 he was captured by left-wing partisans and shot, together with his mistress, Clara Petacci.

Born on 29 July 1883, the son of ardently socialist parents (his father was a blacksmith, his mother a teacher) Benito Mussolini at first had left-wing sympathies. After a short time as a schoolteacher, he spent two years in Switzerland, and in 1909 edited a socialist newspaper. Later, in Milan, he became editor of the socialist newspaper *Avanti* (Forward), and later founded his own publication, *Il Popolo d'Italia* (The People of Italy). When World War I broke out, he at first advocated Italian neutrality, but quickly changed his tune and demanded Italian intervention on the Allied side.

Called up for military service on 15 August 1914, he reached the rank of corporal and was wounded on the Isonzo. He made a full recovery, but was invalided out of the Army and returned to journalism. It was at this point that he began to advocate an extreme form of nationalism and founded the Fascist Party, which he led and expanded with great skill. After his election to Parliament in 1921, the National Fascist Party rapidly gained support, and in October 1922

73

Vice-Admiral Chuichi Nagumo
Japanese Navy

Vice-Admiral Nagumo committed suicide after the last of Japan's remaining naval power was wiped out in the Battle of the Philippine Sea.

Born in 1886, Chuichi Nagumo graduated from the Japanese Naval Academy in 1908. A skilled technician, he specialized in torpedo warfare. Nagumo's talent and energetic approach to naval affairs came to the notice of his superiors, and he rose rapidly up the ladder of promotion, never an easy achievement in the Japanese armed forces. In 1941 Nagumo was in command of the 1st Carrier Division of the 1st Air Fleet, comprising six aircraft-carriers led by his flagship, the *Akagi*, and on 7 December it was this force that launched 374 torpedo-bombers and dive-bombers in the devastating attack on Pearl Harbor. However, although it crippled the American battleship force in the Pacific, the Pearl Harbor operation proved much less profitable to the Japanese than it might have been; the American aircraft-carriers, around which future task forces would be built, were not in port, and shore installations and fuel tanks were left intact.

Nagumo led the same carrier force in a sortie into the Indian Ocean in March 1942, attacking the island of Ceylon, and in June his carrier air power formed the spearhead of a planned attack on the island of Midway. The plan was to bring the surviving American naval forces to battle and destroy them, after which it was anticipated that some form of peace settlement might be negotiated; instead, Nagumo lost his four fleet carriers to US naval air strikes, and with them the war in the Pacific. Thereafter, Nagumo's personal decline was swift. Prematurely aged, he lost his powers of decision and readily agreed to the suggestions of his subordinates, often with disastrous results. He was appointed to command the Central Pacific Fleet, with the task of defending the Marianas. The result was another disaster for the Japanese, with most of their remaining naval air power being destroyed in the Battle of the Philippine Sea. When American forces successfully landed on the island of Saipan, a strategically important base that brought their B-29 bombers within range of the Japanese home islands, Vice-Admiral Nagumo committed suicide on 6 July 1944.

The loss of four fleet carriers at Midway spelt the end of Japanese aspirations in the Pacific, and of Admiral Nagumo.
(National Archives)

Fleet Admiral Chester W. Nimitz
US Navy

A Douglas TBD Devastator pulls away after making a torpedo run on a Japanese carrier in the Battle of Midway. (US Navy)

The man who was to become one of America's most famous admirals, a highly gifted administrator and naval strategist, embarked on a naval career by accident. Born on 24 February 1885 in Fredericksburg, Texas, Chester William Nimitz had his heart set on a career in the US Army, and on graduating from high school he applied to enter the US Military Academy at West Point, only to be informed that there were no vacancies. He therefore sat the entrance examination for the US Naval Academy, Annapolis, and was successful, enrolling in the class of 1905. After graduation he joined the USS *Ohio* and embarked on a cruise to the Far East, being commissioned as an ensign on completion of his two years' sea duty. Returning to the USA, he trained as a submariner, serving in a number of boats before being given command of the Atlantic Submarine Flotilla in 1912.

Chester Nimitz signing the Japanese copy of the Instrument of Surrender on the USS Missouri, Tokyo Bay, 2 September 1945. (US Navy)

Nimitz spent the next year studying diesel engine technology in Germany and Belgium, returning to the USA to spend time as an engineering officer before being appointed Chief of Staff to the Commander Submarines Atlantic. In 1919 he spent a year as Executive Officer of the battleship USS *South Carolina* before returning to the submarine service. In 1933, after various appointments, he was

assigned to his first large ship command, the heavy cruiser USS *Augusta*, which served mostly as flagship of the Asiatic Fleet. In December 1941, after further seagoing and shore appointments, he was designated as Commander-in-Chief, Pacific Fleet, a post in which he served throughout the war.

He took up the appointment immediately after the Japanese attack on Pearl Harbor, and, far from seeking scapegoats he retained all officers in their posts, maintaining that the disaster 'could have happened to anybody' – an act of clemency that did much to restore morale. Nimitz was chiefly responsible for the decisive American victory at Midway and for masterminding the ensuing weakening of Japanese naval strength by ocean-going submarine operations and by the capture of strategic Pacific islands. On 19 December 1944, he was promoted to the newly created rank of Fleet Admiral, and on 2 September 1945 he was the United States signatory to the surrender terms aboard the battleship USS *Missouri* in Tokyo Bay.

Fleet Admiral Chester Nimitz died on 26 February 1966, having spent the post-war years involved in work for the United Nations and the community of San Francisco.

General Sir Richard O'Connor
British Army

Italian soldiers marching cheerfully to war in 1940. General O'Connor's army soon disillusioned them. (author's collection)

The everlasting fame of one of history's forgotten generals, Richard Nugent O'Connor, would have been assured had not political events dictated otherwise. Born in 1899, O'Connor served with distinction during World War I. An open-minded infantryman with a talent for out-manoeuvring the enemy and a keen appreciation of mechanized warfare, he took command of the Western Desert Force in June 1940, the month in which Italy declared war on the side of Germany and began offensive operations against British Commonwealth forces in Cyrenaica. The Italian Desert Army under Marshal Rodolfo Graziani of 250,000 men dwarfed the Western Desert Force's 36,000, but it took two months of insistence by Mussolini before Graziani began his march on Egypt. Long before then, O'Connor's raiding parties had been roving behind Italian lines, shooting up supply columns and destroying fortifications.

Graziani made a cautious advance as far as Sidi Barrani, and ordered his forces to dig in. It was then that O'Connor boldly decided to take the initiative.

In December 1940, with the 4th Indian Division and the 7th Armoured Division, he penetrated the Italian lines and took the enemy completely by surprise, smashing Graziani's forces and chasing them into Libya in a two-day battle that ended the immediate threat to Egypt. In January 1941 the Western Desert Force, now renamed XIII Corps, swept on to win a decisive battle at Beda Fomm, utterly destroying the Italian Tenth Army. In ten weeks, O'Connor's forces had taken 130,000 prisoners, 400 tanks, 1,290 guns and 1,000 trucks.

Then came the blow. The British forces in North Africa were stripped of men and materiel for the futile campaign in Greece, and General Rommel's Afrika Korps arrived to take part in the desert war, throwing the British back into Egypt. General O'Connor was captured, purely by chance, and languished in an Italian POW camp until his release in 1943, when Italy surrendered. He was subsequently given command of the British VIII Corps, which fought in north-west Europe after D-Day.

General O'Connor died in 1981.

Air Chief Marshal Sir Keith Park
Royal Air Force

'If it had not been for Keith Park's conduct in the battle, and his loyalty to me as his Commander-in-Chief, we should not be here today.'

So spoke Lord Dowding, C-in-C RAF Fighter Command during the Battle of Britain, of Air Chief Marshal Sir Keith Park, who commanded No. 11 Group in the forefront of the battle. As history has shown, they were no idle words.

Keith Rodney Park was born in Thames, New Zealand, in 15 June 1892, and was educated at the Otago Boys' High School, Dunedin, and King's College, Auckland. He obtained a post with the Union Steamship Company, but enlisted as a private in the New Zealand Field Artillery on the outbreak of World War I, seeing service in Egypt and at Gallipoli. Commissioned, he was sent to England in time to take part in the first battle of the Somme in July 1916, when he was wounded. Classed 'fit for Home Service only' by the Army, he applied for a transfer to the Royal Flying Corps, and in 1917 he returned to France with No. 48 Squadron, flying Bristol F2B Fighters. By the end of the war he had risen to the rank of major and destroyed twenty enemy aircraft, being awarded the MC and DFC.

Granted a permanent commission, Park commanded Nos 25 and 111 Squadrons in the 1920s, and in 1935, as a group captain, he was appointed Air Attaché in Buenos Aires, Argentina. In 1937 he spent a year as aide-de-camp to King George VI, and in 1938, with the rank of air commodore, he was posted to Fighter Command HQ as Senior Air Staff Officer to the AOC-in-C, Air Marshal Hugh Dowding. Early in 1940 Park was promoted to air vice-marshal and given command of No. 11 Group Fighter Command, whose airfields were spread in a defensive arc south-east of London, and throughout the period of the Battle of Britain he conducted the air defence of his area with masterly skill, supported by the commander of the adjacent No. 10 Group, Air Vice-Marshal Quintin Brand (but not by AVM Trafford Leigh-Mallory, the commander of No. 12 Group north of the Thames, with whom he was constantly at odds).

Ironically, it was Leigh-Mallory who took over No. 11 Group when Park was relieved late in 1940 and posted to command a flying training group. In 1942 he was appointed as AOC Egypt, and was then assigned to command Malta's air defences, where he once again directed defensive operations with a masterly touch. He received a knighthood in 1942, and in 1944 became Air Officer Commanding-in-Chief, Middle East Command. After barely a year in this post he was appointed as AOC-in-C South-East Asia Command, a capacity in which he directed the RAF's final onslaught against the Japanese in South-East Asia. In 1946, he was promoted to air chief marshal.

Sir Keith Park retired from the RAF in 1946 and returned to New Zealand in 1948 to become the South Pacific Director for the Hawker Siddeley Group, whom he had represented in South America for a short period. He died on 6 February 1975.

Air Chief Marshal Sir Keith Park as AOC-in-C, South-East Asia Command. (IWM)

General Alexander Patch
US Army

Early in 1942, when a major-general, Alexander McCarrell Patch, who had commanded a machine-gun battalion in World War I, was appointed commander of the task force dispatched to help the French in New Caledonia; he subsequently organized a formation known as the Americal (American-Caledonian) Division, the only unnumbered division in the United States Army, elements of which took part in the US Army's first offensive operations of the Pacific war, at Guadalcanal on 13 October 1942. In December, Patch was appointed commander of all US forces on Guadalcanal and Tulagi, directing them in the battles of 1943 that ended with the expulsion of the Japanese.

On 2 March 1944, Patch succeeded General Mark Clark as commander of the US Seventh Army in Sicily, moving his headquarters to Naples shortly afterwards. Planning was well advanced for the Allied invasion of southern France (Operation Anvil), which was originally to have been launched in conjunction with the planned landings in Normandy (Operation Overlord), and Patch requested the immediate designation of the American divisions that were to be committed. However, it was soon realized that, because of projected offensives in Italy and the wholesale transfer of landing craft from the Mediterranean to Britain in readiness for 'Overlord', 'Anvil' could not be launched before late July at the very earliest.

In fact it was launched on 15 August 1944, by which time it had been renamed Operation Dragoon. Lieutenant-General Patch led the Seventh Army in the liberation of the French Riviera, and then in a brilliantly executed advance through southern Europe. In December, it became the first of the Allied armies to reach the Rhine. In conjunction with General Patton's Third Army, it occupied the Saar and then pushed on across the Rhine to take Munich and Nuremberg. On 4 May 1945 it made contact with General Mark Clark's Fifth Army, pushing up through Austria.

After the war, General Patch was placed in command of the US Fourth Army at Fort Sam Houston, Texas. On 21 November 1945, he died of a heart attack in San Antonio, aged only 55.

In 1944, General Patch led the US Seventh Army in the invasion of Southern France and the subsequent advance into Germany. (National Archives)

General George S. Patton
US Army

General Patton pictured soon after assuming command of the US Third Army. (National Archives)

George Smith Patton was born in St Gabriel, California, on 11 November 1885 into a family with a long military tradition. He was educated at the Virginia Military Institute, and in 1909 he graduated from the US Military Academy, West Point, being commissioned into the 15th Cavalry . In 1916 he was appointed aide-de-camp to General Pershing during the latter's expedition against Mexico. Patton accompanied Pershing when the latter was given command of the US Expeditionary Force in World War I, and was one of the first officers assigned to the newly formed US Army Tanks Corps, being given the task of organizing and training the 1st tank brigade. His experience as a tank officer in the St-Mihiel offensive and in the Meuse-Argonne sector in September 1918, when he was wounded, led him to appreciate the tank's potential against static defence formations.

After various assignments between the wars, Patton was given command of the 2nd Armored Division in 1941, with the rank of major-general, and early in 1942 he took command of the 1st Armored Corps. He played an important part in the Allied landings in North Africa in November 1942, commanding the ground elements of the Western Task Force that entered French Morocco, and in March 1943 he was given command of the US II Corps with the task of restoring its morale after its shattering defeat in the Kasserine Pass, Tunisia. In July 1943, as a lieutenant-general, he led the US 7th Army in the assault on Sicily. His anti-British attitudes, his personal dislike of Montgomery and his indiscreet political pronouncements led to his being reprimanded by Eisenhower, the Allied Supreme Commander. His ruin was nearly brought about when, visiting a hospital, he slapped a shell-shocked soldier and accused him of cowardice. He was quickly recalled to Britain and given command of a non-existent army 'formed' for diversionary purposes in East Anglia prior to Operation Overlord.

He was again given active command following the Allied landings in Normandy in June 1944, and distinguished himself by leading the US 3rd Army from the breakout at Avranches in August 1944 in a race to the Seine and then the Meuse, which was halted only through shortage of fuel. In December 1944, his army moved at great speed to relieve German pressure on Bradley's formations during the Ardennes offensive. This accomplished, Patton's next attacks took him across the Rhine, with the loss of only 34 men killed or wounded. Finally, he pushed down the Danube into Austria and Czechoslovakia. However, his policy of destroying any village that offered even the slightest resistance to his advance once again brought him into disrepute, and distrust of his judgement intensified when he advocated that the Western Allies should attack the Soviet armies in the East to prevent their seizure of large areas of Germany.

After the war, Patton was made military governor of Bavaria as a four-star general and assigned to command the 15th Army, which was little more than a headquarters. Seriously injured in an automobile accident near Mannheim, he died in hospital on 21 December 1945.

Generalfeldmarschall Friedrich Paulus
German Army

Friedrich Paulus was born in Breitenau, Hesse, on 23 September 1890. He was educated in Kassel and read law at Marburg University before being commissioned into the 3rd Infantry Regiment in 1910. At the outbreak of World War I he was adjutant of the 3rd Battalion, subsequently serving in various staff posts. At the end of the war he was a Hauptmann, with the Iron Cross, 1st Class. He remained in the Army, reaching the rank of Major in 1931, and in 1935 he was appointed Chief of Staff of the newly formed Mechanized Troops Command in Berlin. In 1938 he became Chief of Staff of the XVI Army Corps, the first German armoured corps. August 1939 found him in command of the 10th Army in Leipzig, which was redesignated 6th Army before the campaign in France.

In April and May 1941 Paulus was sent by Hitler to supervise the activities of Erwin Rommel's Deutsches Afrika Corps, cautioning Rommel against taking the offensive too soon, before the replenishment of his forces was assured. In January 1942 he took command of the 6th Army, which was then near Kharkov in the Ukraine. During the German summer offensive, the 6th Army drove eastwards through the steppes towards the Volga, pushing on to Stalingrad. There, in November, a counter-offensive by the Red Army resulted in his forces being encircled. Attempts by the Luftwaffe to resupply the German forces failed, as did an attempt by the 4th Panzer Army to break through and extricate the 6th Army. In January 1943 Hitler raised Paulus to the rank of field marshal, on the basis that no German field marshal had ever surrendered; but Paulus, his ammunition and supplies exhausted, had no alternative. On 2 February 1943 he capitulated, and 90,000 German troops – the remnant of the 220,000 with which he had begun the march to Stalingrad – went into captivity.

In captivity, Paulus joined the National Committee for a Free Germany, a Soviet-sponsored organization, and called on his fellow Germans to surrender. In 1946 he was summoned to the Nuremberg War Crimes Trials as a witness for the prosecution. On his release from Soviet custody in 1953 he settled in Dresden, where he died on 1 February 1957.

Friedrich Paulus might have saved the German 6th Army, had he defied Hitler and ordered a breakout from Stalingrad. (Bundesarchiv)

Lieutenant-General Sir Arthur Percival
British Army

Lieutenant-General Percival, on the far right, and members of his staff surrendering to the Japanese at Singapore. (IWM)

Born in 1887, Arthur Percival was commissioned into the Bedfordshire Regiment and served with distinction in France during World War I, being awarded the DSO, MC and the French Croix de Guerre. In 1919 he volunteered for service in North Russia with the Royal Fusiliers, and later served with the Essex Regiment in Ireland. Various staff appointments between the wars brought him steady promotion, until in 1939 he was a divisional commander with the rank of major-general. In April 1941 he was appointed General Officer Commanding, Malaya, his principal task being to defend the strategic base of Singapore.

The defensive problems that confronted Percival were complex. The seaward-orientated heavy guns of Singapore meant that any move on the island fortress by the Japanese would have to be made from the north, through the Malayan peninsula, so the denial of landing beaches and airfields in the north, across the border in Thailand, was essential to the defence of Malaya. The British wished, if possible, to avoid a war with Japan, so no attempt was made to move into southern Thailand in order to occupy key positions. At the same time, the British were not prepared to abandon northern Malaya and concentrate their forces on Singapore, so on the eve of war their position was one of dispersal and weakness.

On 8 December 1941, Japanese forces landed unopposed at Singora and Patani, on the Gulf of Siam. On the other hand, a landing at Kota Bahru, in Malaya, was fiercely opposed and nearly came to grief. It was the forces attacking from Thailand that slashed their way through the British defences in the north to advance on Singapore, concentrating three divisions for the assault on the island. Despite vigorous defensive fighting by Australian, British and Indian troops, Lieutenant-General Percival was compelled to surrender on 15 February 1942, and 130,000 British and Commonwealth troops were taken prisoner in the biggest single defeat ever suffered by the British Army.

Percival was blamed for the loss of Singapore, but in reality his hands were tied by political indecision and a lack of modern equipment, particularly in the air. Once the Japanese had established total air superiority, there was no longer any possibility that Singapore might hold out. Percival was released from Japanese captivity in 1945, and at the request of General Douglas MacArthur witnessed the Japanese sign the instrument of surrender on the USS *Missouri* in Tokyo Bay on 2 September. He died in 1966.

The destruction of Germany's cities was a policy devised by Sir Charles Portal, and implemented by 'Bomber' Harris. This was Cologne. (author's collection)

Born on 21 May 1893, Charles Frederick Algernon Portal was educated at Winchester and Oxford, where he read for a law degree with the intention of becoming a barrister, an ambition he never fulfilled. On the outbreak of World War I he enlisted in the Royal Engineers, serving as a corporal before being commissioned. In July 1915 he transferred to the Royal Flying Corps, training first as an observer and later as a pilot. After flying Morane Bullets with No. 60 Squadron, he became a flight commander with No. 3 Squadron, flying BE.2cs, and in June 1917 he was given command of No. 16 Squadron, flying R.E.8 army co-operation aircraft. In January 1919 he became CO of No. 1 Wing.

In 1922 'Peter' Portal, as he was known, attended the first course at the new RAF Staff College, Cranwell. In 1927, now a wing commander, he was appointed to command No. 7 Squadron, flying Vickers Virginia heavy bombers. His assignments in the 1930s included Officer Commanding, Aden Command (1934) and Air member for Personnel (1939). In April 1940 he was appointed Air Officer Commanding-in-Chief, RAF Bomber Command, a position that brought him a knighthood, and in October that year he became Chief of the Air Staff, a post he was to retain throughout World War II.

It was during his tour at Bomber Command that the seeds of area bombing, the concept of which was later unjustly attributed to 'Bomber' Harris (although he implemented it), were sown in Portal's mind, although his assessment of how such a policy might be carried out was unrealistic; he believed that a force of 4,000–6,000 heavy bombers might kill 900,000 German civilians and seriously injure a million more, and said so in a document that was later to cause much controversy and outrage.

A cold and somewhat remote figure, Portal nevertheless proved himself to be a brilliant Chief of Staff, despite being surrounded by officers who were mostly older than himself. He earned the admiration of Churchill, and he won the confidence and respect of the Americans, a tremendously important point in a war where so much depended on inter-Allied co-operation.

Marshal of the RAF Viscount Portal retired from the RAF in 1945, and in the post-war years, as Controller, Atomic Energy, was heavily involved in the development of British nuclear weapons. In 1960 he was appointed Chairman of the British Aircraft Corporation. In 1970 he was diagnosed as having an incurable cancer, and died on 22 April 1971.

German civilians in the ruins of Berlin, 1945. (author's collection)

Admiral of the Fleet Sir Dudley Pound
Royal Navy

Born in 1877, Alfred Dudley Pickman Rogers Pound, who rose to be First Sea Lord in 1939, had the unenviable task of steering the Royal Navy through its years of crisis, when the Battle of the Atlantic hung in the balance and Britain was hard pressed to retain its naval supremacy in the Mediterranean. It was to Admiral Pound's everlasting credit that, during those dangerous years, the Royal Navy rose to every demand that was made upon it, overstretched though its resources were. He also succeeded in gaining the complete confidence of Winston Churchill, who stepped from the office of First Lord of the Admiralty to become Prime Minister in May 1940, and he was able to head off some of the more dangerous and unrealistic projects dreamed up by Churchill in the early months of his premiership, such as the occupation of the Mediterranean islands of Pantelleria and the Dodecanese.

Pound shrewdly analysed the principal naval threats to Britain's survival. In 1939–40, for example, he identified the principal menace to Britain's lifelines as being, not enemy submarines, which were then deployed only in relatively small numbers, but the major German surface warships, which had the ability to paralyse the British supply system and seaborne trade. Hunting them down became Pound's top priority, and the Navy gained an early success in December 1939, when the German pocket battleship *Admiral Graf Spee* was driven into Montevideo harbour by British and New Zealand warships and scuttled. This was followed, in May 1941, by the destruction of the *Bismarck*, the world's most powerful battleship.

Admiral Pound was also opposed to sending convoys to Russia in the summer months of 1942, when conditions of almost continuous daylight prevailed in the Arctic. He was overruled by the War Cabinet, under heavy pressure from President Roosevelt, and as a consequence the convoys suffered disastrous losses to U-boats and aircraft. He also opposed Churchill's desire to redeploy most of the Eastern Fleet's warships to the Mediterranean, which would have left the Indian Ocean wide open to attack by even a modest Japanese raiding force.

In the summer of 1943, Admiral Pound finally succumbed to the stress of leadership, suffering a stroke while in Canada for a conference. He died on 21 October that year, the date that marks the anniversary of the Battle of Trafalgar.

Admiral Sir Dudley Pound accompanied by Winston Churchill, who at this time was First Lord of the Admiralty. (Royal Navy) 83

Grossadmiral Erich Raeder
German Navy

Erich Raeder was born in Wandsbek, near Hamburg, in 1876, and joined the Imperial German Navy as a cadet in 1894, being commissioned as a Leutnant three years later. In 1910–12 he served as navigation officer on the Kaiser's yacht *Hohenzollern*, and for most of World War I he served on various cruisers, taking part in the Battle of the Dogger Bank in 1915 and being given command of the light cruiser *Coln* in 1918. In 1920, as a captain, he entered the Reichswehr and worked in the Naval Archives, where he was assigned the task of writing a two-volume work on the war at sea, with particular reference to commerce raiders in distant waters, and it was only while compiling this account that he became aware of the damage these vessels had inflicted on Allied shipping, something that would greatly influence his naval strategy at a later date.

In 1922 Raeder was appointed Inspector of the Naval Training Department, in 1924 he was in command of German light naval forces in the North Sea, and in 1925 he took charge of the Baltic Station. From 1928 to 1935 he was Chief of the Naval Staff,

in which post he enthusiastically welcomed Hitler's rearmament plans. As Supreme Naval Commander from 1935, he instigated an intensive building programme of battleships, battlecruisers, heavy cruisers and armoured ships, popularly known as pocket battleships, designed specifically for commerce raiding, and of submarines, whose role would be to starve Britain into submission and so avoid a costly naval confrontation on the style of the Battle of Jutland in 1916.

From the outset of World War II he advocated the concentration of all Germany's naval resources against Britain, and spoke out against a war on two fronts, which brought him into confrontation with Hitler. When the latter considered scrapping the German Navy's remaining surface ships in 1943, and using their heavy guns for coastal defence, Raeder resigned and was replaced by Karl Doenitz.

In 1946 Grossadmiral Erich Raeder was tried as a war criminal and sentenced to life imprisonment, but was released in 1955. He subsequently wrote two volumes of his memoirs, and died in Kiel on 6 November 1960.

A naval officer of the old school, Erich Raeder believed that the path to victory lay in commerce raiding. (Bundesarchiv)

Admiral Sir Bertram H. Ramsay
Royal Navy

*Admiral Ramsay masterminded the Dunkirk
evacuation in May 1940, and played a key role in
planning subsequent amphibious operations.*
(Royal Navy)

The son of an army officer, Bertram Home Ramsay was born in London on 20 January 1883. He joined the Royal Navy, and after training as a midshipman on HMS *Britannica* he joined the cruiser HMS *Crescent*. He was mentioned in dispatches for his part in an action in Somaliland in 1903–4, and promoted lieutenant. During World War I, Ramsay held commands in the Dover Patrol, and later became Naval ADC to King George V. He retired from the Royal Navy in 1938, with the rank of rear-admiral, but was recalled to duty on the outbreak of World War II and appointed Flag Officer, Dover.

When the Germans struck in France and the Low Countries, Ramsay was made responsible for the evacuation of key personnel, including the Dutch Royal Family, from the Hook of Holland to England; but his truly notable achievement was in overseeing the huge naval effort that resulted in the evacuation of a third of a million British and French troops from Dunkirk and other ports on the French coast. He was subsequently knighted and promoted admiral. In November 1942, as deputy to Admiral Cunningham, he was responsible for organizing the Allied landings in Algeria (Operation Torch), and during the invasion of Sicily in July 1943 he commanded the Eastern Naval Task Force, controlling 795 warships and transports and 713 landing craft.

In December 1943 Ramsay was appointed Allied Naval Commander for the forthcoming invasion of Normandy, a tremendous undertaking involving the handling and control of 2,730 vessels of all types. The work he put into planning the operation was stupendous; the final plan for Operation Neptune, as the naval part of the operation was code-named, was a document running to over 700 foolscap pages, presented to the naval authorities on 10 April 1944. After the invasion was successfully completed, he oversaw the occupation by the Allies of the northern French ports.

Admiral Sir Bertram Ramsay was killed on 2 January 1945, when the aircraft in which he was travelling to a conference crashed on take-off at Toussus-le-Noble, France.

Marshal Konstantin Rokossovsky
Soviet Army

One of the most able commanders of World War II, Konstantin Rokossovsky was fortunate to survive Stalin's infamous purges. (via J. R. Cavanagh)

Konstantin Rokossovsky has been described, with some justification, as one of the most able commanders of World War II. Born in Warsaw in 1896, he served in the Tsarist Army in World War I, but switched to the Red Guard at the time of the Russian Revolution and fought with the cavalry during the Civil War. In the inter-war years he advocated 'radical' concepts, such as mechanized warfare. A victim of the Stalinist purge of 1937, he survived, despite being badly beaten, and in May 1940, when the Red Army was reorganized, he was released from captivity and rehabilitated, being given command of the 19th Mechanized Corps near Kiev.

When the Germans attacked in May 1941, the 19th Corps was quickly overwhelmed by the ferocity of the onslaught, but Rokossovsky carried out an effective fighting retreat to Smolensk, and at one point assumed command of the remnants of two Soviet armies. Early in October he was given command of the Sixteenth Army, with orders to hold key defensive positions on the approach to Moscow, which it successfully did. In January 1942 Rokossovsky was wounded and put out of action until July, when he was given command of the Bryansk Front in the Stalingrad sector. Two months later, his command was organized into the Don Front, and it was this formation that he led in attacks from the north-east to link up with the South-West Front and complete the encirclement of the German Sixth Army.

In February 1943, with the Sixth Army destroyed,

Rokossovsky took over the new Central Front and began the drive towards Kursk. In July 1943, it was Rokossovsky's units that bore the brunt of the German assault on the Kursk salient. After the battle, which resulted in the destruction of the cream of the German armour, Rokossovsky's forces pursued the enemy to the Dniester river, poised for an attack into the Ukraine.

Early in 1944 Rokossovsky took command of the Byelorussian Front, which forged on into Poland – and halted on the Vistula while the Germans smashed the Warsaw Uprising. Early in 1945 his armies swung north to cut off the German forces in East Prussia. Rokossovsky's command was not involved in the battle for Berlin; instead, it pushed along the north German coast to link up with British forces at Wismar on 5 May 1945.

In 1949 Rokossovsky was made Commander-in-Chief and Minister of Defence in Poland, and in 1952 he became Deputy Prime Minister. Recalled to the Soviet Union in 1956, he subsequently served two terms as Deputy Minister of Defence.

Marshal Konstantin 'Steel Teeth' Rokossovsky died in 1968.

Konstantin Rokossovsky pictured in his command post on the Russian Front, 1944. (via J. R. Cavanagh)

Generalfeldmarschall Erwin Rommel
German Army

Born on 15 November 1891, in the small Württemberg town of Heidenheim, near Ulm, the son of a local schoolmaster, Erwin Johannes Eugen Rommel was destined to become one of the most famous generals of all time. Commissioned into the 124th Infantry Regiment in 1912, he fought on the Western Front and in Romania during World War I, being wounded several times and awarded the Iron Cross and the Pour le Mérite. By the end of the war he was a Hauptmann, and as a member of the post-war Reichswehr he commanded a company of the 13th Infantry Regiment for the next nine years. In 1932 he was promoted Major, and after 1933 he soon came to the attention of Adolf Hitler, who appointed Rommel to command the Führer's escort battalion during the occupation of the Sudetenland and Czechoslovakia.

In September 1939, now a Generalmajor, Rommel was made responsible for Hitler's safety when the latter visited front-line units during the invasion of Poland. During this campaign, Rommel witnessed at first hand the deadly

One of the most famous generals of all time, Erwin Rommel conducted his desert campaign with limited resources. (Bundesarchiv)

effectiveness of air power and armour working in concert, and he requested a fighting command in charge of an armoured division. Against opposition from certain senior officers, who complained that Rommel had no experience of armoured warfare, he was given command of the 7th Panzer Division, which he led in an epic dash to the English Channel coast during the Blitzkrieg of May 1940.

In February 1941 Rommel arrived in North Africa in command of the Deutsches Afrika Korps, and it was here that his real legend was born, as the brilliant tactician who became known as the 'Desert Fox'. Although much of his success was due to the monitoring of British signals traffic by the Italians, he showed enormous audacity and flair in conducting first an offensive, and then a defensive, campaign against vastly superior numbers. A courageous officer, Rommel always led from the front, and his chivalry became a byword on both sides of the front.

Following the Axis defeat in North Africa, Rommel was placed in charge of the 'West Wall' defences on the Channel coast, and set about strengthening them in readiness to fight off an Allied invasion, but he never received anything like the amount of material he needed. On 31 December 1943 he was placed in command of Army Group B, and was still in command when the Allies invaded Normandy on 6 June 1944. Rommel, realizing that Normandy was lost, wanted to set up a new defensive line on the river Orne, but Hitler would not hear of it.

On 17 July, his staff car was strafed by Allied fighters and he was thrown into the road, sustaining severe head injuries. During his time in hospital, he came under suspicion for having been implicated in the 20 July bomb plot against Hitler. The allegation was false, but on 14 October he was visited by two officers from Berlin, who gave him the stark choice of facing charges of conspiracy in court, or of committing suicide. To protect his family from disgrace, he chose the latter course, taking poison at noon that day. In a final lie, the Nazis told the German people that Rommel, who had remained utterly loyal to Hitler to the very end, had succumbed to his wounds.

Franklin D. Roosevelt
US President

Franklin Delano Roosevelt was the only man to be elected to the office of President of the United States four times. Born in 1882, his early career was in law, but in 1910 he was elected to the New York State Senate. Roosevelt, a Democrat, allied himself with reform groups inside the party. Between 1913 and 1920 he served as Assistant Secretary of the Navy, building up a reputation as a sound administrator. Despite being stricken by poliomyelitis and barely able to walk for the rest of his life, in 1928 he won the governorship of New York State, and in 1932, having been chosen as presidential candidate by the Democratic Party, he succeeded the Republican Herbert C. Hoover as President of the United States. His immediate, daunting task was to address the worst effects of the Depression, to which end he rushed various fiscal measures through Congress and established a number of government agencies, notably the National Recovery Administration. Strenuous efforts were also made to develop the country's natural resources, with the establishment of such bodies as the Tennessee Valley Authority in 1933. The success of these and other measures, which were part of what Roosevelt called his 'New Deal', led to his re-election in 1936.

Roosevelt had a shrewd appreciation of diplomacy and foreign affairs, cultivating a 'good neighbour' policy with the countries of Latin America and denouncing the growing power and aggressive aims of Germany and Italy. The expansionist policy of Japan was of particular concern, leading to the eventual imposition of sanctions. At the outbreak of war in Europe, although the United States remained neutral, Roosevelt declared that the USA's military output would be an 'arsenal for democracy', and large orders for aircraft and other war material were soon being placed by purchasing commissions from Britain and France. He was again elected President in 1940. In 1941, against much opposition, Roosevelt forced the Lend-Lease Act through Congress, paving the way for the supply of war material in unprecedented quantities to Britain in return for the use of British bases in the Caribbean.

In August 1941, Roosevelt and Winston Churchill met at sea and drafted the Atlantic Charter, an historic document providing for the joint safety of their respective nations in the face of German aggression. Four months later, the USA was brought into the war when the Japanese attacked Pearl Harbor, and thereafter Roosevelt devoted his considerable energies almost exclusively to the conflict, authorizing massive increases in the strength of the US armed forces. Despite his growing poor health he attended all the international conferences with the other Allied leaders, and worked tirelessly for the establishment of the United Nations. He was re-elected for a fourth term as President in November 1944, but died from a cerebral haemorrhage on 12 April 1945, only a month before the end of the war in Europe. He was succeeded by his vice-president, Harry S. Truman.

US President Franklin Delano Roosevelt overcame much Congressional opposition to supply Britain with war material.
(National Archives)

Marshal Pavel Rotmistrov
Soviet Army

A Soviet T-34 tank in flames. Rotmistrov's policy of engaging the enemy at close quarters caused huge Russian tank losses.
(Bundesarchiv)

Born in 1901, Pavel Rotmistrov joined the Red Army in 1919 and fought in the ranks during the Russian Civil War. He attended a command school in 1924 and became a platoon commander, rising to battalion command in 1931, when he attended the Frunze Military Academy. From 1931 to 1937 he served in divisional and army HQs and commanded a rifle regiment. During the Russo-Finnish war of 1939–40 he commanded a tank battalion, and was appointed Chief of Staff of the 35th Tank Brigade.

In May 1941 he became Chief of Staff of the 3rd Mechanized Corps, one of the large and unwieldy armoured formations that were quickly disrupted and destroyed as the experienced German Panzer divisions tore into Soviet territory in June. In September, Rotmistrov was given command of the 8th (later 3rd Guards) Tank Brigade, which was involved in heavy fighting at Staraya Russa, Rogachev and then in the counter-offensive at Moscow. From April 1942 he commanded the 7th Tank (later 3rd Guards Tank) Corps, one of the first powerful armoured formations to be reintroduced after the battle for Moscow. As its commander, he saw service at Stalingrad. In January 1943 the Corps was in action against von Manstein's counter-

offensive, and took part in the recapture of Rostov.

In February 1943 Rotmistrov was assigned to the command of the 5th Guards Tank Army, which saw action at Prokhorovka during the Battle of Kursk in June 1943, the biggest tank battle of the war. Since the guns of the German tanks outranged his own, Rotmistrov ordered his tank commanders to engage the enemy at close quarters, regardless of losses. He continued to lead the 5th Guards Tank Army as the armoured spearhead of the Voronezh, 2nd Ukrainian and 3rd Byelorussian Fronts, being appointed deputy commander of the Soviet Armoured and Mechanized Forces from August 1944.

After the war, Rotmistrov commanded the armoured and mechanized forces of the Soviet group of Forces in Germany, and later in the Far East. From 1948 to 1958 he taught at the General Staff Academy, and from 1958 was head of the Tank Academy. From 1964 to 1968 he was deputy Minister of defence, and was then a senior Inspector-General of the Armed Forces, with the rank of Chief Marshal of Armour.

Pavel Rotmistrov was without doubt one of the best armoured commanders of World War II. He died in 1982.

Generalfeldmarschall Gerd von Rundstedt
German Army

Gerd von Rundstedt had a see-saw career, being dismissed on the whim of Adolf Hitler and then reinstated. (Bundesarchiv)

The son of a Prussian Generalmajor, Gerd von Rundstedt was born in Aschersleben, Saxony, on 12 December 1875, and by 1893, following in his father's footsteps, he was an officer in the Prussian infantry. In 1912 he was appointed a company commander in the 171st Infantry Regiment, and during World War I he served as a general staff officer in Turkey and France, specializing in large-scale tactical manoeuvres. In 1919 he was serving in the post-war Reichswehr, and in the following year, as an Oberstleutnant, he was made Chief of Staff of the 3rd Cavalry Division at Weimar. Promoted to general officer rank in 1927, he served in various appointments until 1938, when he resigned, largely as a result of his belief that the Wehrmacht was not ready to go to war.

In 1939 he was recalled to duty and given command of Army Group South in the invasion of Poland. In 1940 he was placed in command of Army Group A for the invasion of France, conducting a brilliantly successful offensive through the Ardennes; in September, in recognition of his services, he was awarded the Knight's Cross and promoted to Generalfeldmarschall. He had been designated to command the invasion of England, but this was abandoned and instead, in June 1941, he was given command of Army Group South in its drive through the Ukraine. In November, however, he was dismissed by Hitler when he advocated a strategic withdrawal to shorten the German front.

Reinstated in March 1942, he was appointed Commander-in-Chief West, in charge of Army Group D, with responsibility for all German defences from the Netherlands to the Spanish frontier. After the defences failed to stop the Allied invasion in June 1944, he was again dismissed, and replaced by Generalfeldmarschall von Kluge. Recalled yet again as C-in-C West in September, he recognized the peril of the German position and urged Hitler to end the war, a proposal that resulted in another dismissal. In January 1945 he was given nominal command of the Ardennes offensive, which by then had been halted, and after its failure, and the capture of the vital Rhine bridge at Remagen in March, he resigned his command. He was captured by the Americans at Bad Tolz on 1 May and handed over to the British, who indicted him for war crimes. He never stood trial because of his ill-health, and was released in 1949. He died in Hanover on 24 February 1953.

General Wladyslaw Sikorski
Polish Statesman

Born in Galicia in 1881, Wladyslaw Sikorski was educated at the universities of Krakow and Lvov, where he studied engineering. In 1908 he founded a nationalist military organization, which fought with the Austrian Army against the Russians in World War I. He served in the Polish-Soviet war of 1920–21, and in the latter year was appointed Chief of the Polish General Staff. In 1922 Sikorski was appointed Prime Minister of Poland, a post he held for a year. In 1924–5 he was Minister of Military Affairs, being responsible for upgrading the Polish armed forces, but in 1926, following the rise to power of Josef Pilsudski, he was forced to resign from his military command. In 1939, when the Germans invaded Poland, Sikorski established a government in exile in London; this was recognized and supported by all the Allied powers, although the Soviet Union broke off diplomatic relations in 1943, following allegations (which were later substantiated) that the Russians had murdered several thousand Polish officers at Katyn, near Smolensk, following the Soviet occupation of the eastern part of Poland.

Sikorski and his lieutenants in exile performed sterling work for the Allied cause, raising an army of 10,000 men in Great Britain; but Poland and its dealings with Britain and America remained one of the major problems of World War II. President Roosevelt and Prime Minister Winston Churchill both wanted the Polish Government in Exile to form the basis of a free and democratic government in post-war Poland, but the obstacles in the path of this ideal sometimes seemed insurmountable. There was, for example, the question of Poland's post-war boundaries. Poland's frontier in the east was to be the so-called Curzon Line, with some corrections in Poland's favour; for example, any Polish territory lost to the USSR would be amply compensated for by former German territory in the west. Churchill, however, failed in his aim to secure a rapid agreement from the Poles, and the problem intensified when Sikorski, whom Churchill greatly respected and admired, was killed in an air crash at Gibraltar in July 1943. He was replaced by the left-wing Stanislaw Mikolajczyk, who was pro-Russian and consequently distrusted by many of his ministerial colleagues.

The story of Poland in the immediate post-war years might have been different, had Sikorski survived the war.

Sturmbannführer Otto Skorzeny
German Army

The man who was to become one of Hitler's most daring and ruthless soldiers, Otto Skorzeny, was born on 12 June 1908 into a typical middle-class Viennese family, and studied engineering at the University of Vienna. He joined the embryo Nazi Party in the 1920s and became a member of the Waffen SS. In the early part of World War II he proved himself to be an excellent soldier and quickly rose through the ranks to become an officer. He participated in the assault on the West in 1940, the invasion of the Balkans, and finally in the invasion of Russia, where he was wounded in 1941 and sent home to convalesce. Returning to action, he received the Iron Cross in 1942. In April 1943 he was promoted to Hauptsturmführer (Captain) and named as commander of Germany's special forces. It was now that his rise to fame really began.

In July 1943, Adolf Hitler learned that his ally Benito Mussolini had been overthrown and placed under arrest following the Allied invasion of Sicily. Hitler's intention was to return Mussolini to power as leader of a puppet government in northern Italy, and he personally ordered Skorzeny to effect a rescue. For a month, Skorzeny's intelligence resources tracked Mussolini across Italy, and finally established that he was being held captive in the Albergo Rifugio, a resort high in the Gran Sasso mountains. Skorzeny at once assembled a force of

seventy crack paratroops at Practica di Mare airfield, south of Rome, and on 12 September flew them to the target area in DFS 230 gliders, which crash-landed on the rocky slopes. It took just four minutes for the paratroops to overcome slight resistance and free Mussolini, who was flown to Practica di Marc in a Fieseler Storch light aircraft and from there to Hitler's headquarters at Berchtesgaden. Skorzeny's reward for this daring mission was a Knight's Cross and further promotion.

Although Skorzeny is associated chiefly with the rescue of Mussolini and with the deployment of English-speaking German soldiers to spread chaos behind American lines during the Ardennes offensive of December 1944, he was also responsible for keeping the Hungarian government loyal to Hitler by occupying its offices and preventing the Hungarian regent, Admiral Horthy, from signing a separate peace with the Russians in 1944.

After the war, Skorzeny escaped from American custody and fled to Argentina, where he organized Juan Peron's police force and acted as personal bodyguard to Eva Peron. He eventually settled in Spain, where he spent his latter years as an engineering consultant; he also made determined efforts to help former SS comrades to escape justice. He died in Madrid in July 1975.

'Scarface' Skorzeny's most spectacular coup of World War II was the rescue of Benito Mussolini in September 1943.

Field Marshal Viscount Slim
British Army

Field Marshal Viscount Slim was deservedly called the finest British commander of World War II. (IWM)

The son of a Bristol iron merchant, William Joseph Slim was born in 1891. On the outbreak of World War I he was commissioned into the Royal Warwickshire Regiment, subsequently seeing action at Gallipoli, on the Western Front and in Mesopotamia. He was wounded twice, and was awarded the Military Cross. Between the wars, Slim spent several years in India with the 6th Gurkha Rifles. In 1934 he attended the Army Staff College at Camberley, graduating a year later to become a lieutenant-colonel.

At the outbreak of World War II Slim was a brigade commander in the 5th Indian Division, stationed in Eritrea, East Africa. By May 1941, now a major-general, he was commanding the 10th Indian Division. In March 1942, Slim was posted to Burma, where Allied forces were in danger of being put to flight by the Japanese. In Command of I Burma Corps, and enlisting the aid of his Chinese allies, he turned a potential rout into a fighting retreat, the longest in the history of the British Army, organizing a series of temporary defensive lines to slow down the enemy's advance to the border with India.

In October 1943 Slim was appointed commander of the Fourteenth Army. Early in 1944 his forces advanced into the Arakan, where they encountered formidable Japanese opposition, but with the help of massive resupply by land and air they turned what might have become a humiliating defeat into a victory. Slim's decisive achievements were his victories over the Japanese Fifteenth Army at Kohima and Imphal (7 March to 22 June 1944), made possible by massive air resupply – something that would not have been possible without total Allied command of the air.

Building on this success, in late 1944 the Fourteenth Army began its advance into Burma. Slim deceived the Japanese into believing that the main axis of the advance would be through central Burma towards Mandalay; in fact, under radio silence, a major part of his forces moved around the south-western flank, breaking the enemy's rail link from Rangoon and capturing Meiktila and Mandalay in an offensive lasting from 14 January to 28 March 1945. On 2 May, Rangoon, the Burmese capital, fell to the Allies. Two months later Slim was promoted general and appointed Commander-in-Chief, Allied Forces South-East Asia. In 1948 he became Chief of the Imperial General Staff and received promotion to field marshal, later serving as Governor-General of Australia from 1953 to 1960. His history of the Burma Campaign, *Defeat into Victory*, published in 1956, was acclaimed as one of the finest accounts to emerge from World War II.

Field Marshal Slim was created a viscount in 1960. He died in 1970.

General Carl A. Spaatz
US Army Air Force

A very experienced pilot, and one of the pioneers of long-range aviation, Carl Spaatz went on to become one of the most famous air commanders of WWII. (National Archives)

Destined to become one of the most famous American air commanders of World War II, Carl Spaatz was born in Boyertown, Pennsylvania, in 1891. Graduating from the US Military Academy, West Point, on 12 June 1914, he was commissioned into the infantry as a 2nd lieutenant and served in Hawaii until October 1915, when he transferred to the US Air Service and trained as a pilot. After serving in Mexico in 1916 he was promoted to captain and went to France with the American Expeditionary Force in command of the 31st Aero Squadron. Transferred to the 2nd Pursuit Group in September 1918, he was credited with the destruction of three enemy fighters in the last weeks of the war, and was awarded the DSC. Back in the United States as a major, he held various commands in the 1920s, and in January 1929, in an early demonstration of flight refuelling, he captained a Fokker C.2 aircraft on a record flight lasting 150 hours 40 minutes and 15 seconds.

In November 1939 Spaatz, now a colonel, joined the office of the Chief of Air Corps, and in the following year he was sent to England as an observer during the Battle of Britain. In 1941 he became Chief of Staff of the new US Army Air Forces, and then Commanding General of the Air Force Combat Command in 1942, when he helped to organize the establishment and deployment of the US 8th Air Force in Britain. Like General Arnold, he was a staunch advocate of strategic bombing, and when General Eisenhower appointed him Theatre Air Officer (Europe) in August 1942, he assumed overall responsibility for American air strategy against Germany and Italy. In December 1942 he

assumed command of the 12th Air Force in North Africa, and in January 1943 he was appointed to the command of the North-West African Air Force, with the rank of lieutenant-general. He subsequently commanded the 15th Air Force in Italy, returning to England in January 1944 to command the US Strategic Air Forces in Europe. Unlike the British, who advocated area bombing, he favoured the bombing of selected targets through precision attacks on industry and communications. This policy necessitated the continued use of daylight attacks and resulted in heavy American losses, which Spaatz strove to minimize by introducing 'boxes' consisting of layers of bombers flying in close formation to increase their defensive firepower. It was not until the introduction of long-range escort fighters, however, that the precision bombing concept began to pay real dividends.

In June 1945 Spaatz, now a general, assumed command of the US Strategic Air Forces in the Pacific, supervising the B-29 attacks on Japan, including the two atomic bomb missions. In February 1946 he was nominated to become commander of the Army Air Forces, and in September 1947 he was appointed as the first Chief of Staff of the new United States Air Force. He retired with the rank of general on 3 June 1948.

General Spaatz died on 14 July 1974, at the age of 83. He was buried at the US Air Force Academy.

Carl Spaatz seen in 1944, when he was Commanding General of the US Strategic Air Forces.

Josef Visarionovich Stalin
Soviet Dictator

Born in Gori, Georgia, in 1879, Stalin, whose original name was Dzhugashvili, was the son of a shoemaker. He studied at Tiflis Orthodox Theological Seminary, from which he was expelled in 1899, the year in which he became a dedicated revolutionary. He was first arrested for conspiracy in 1902. Continuing his subversive activities in the Caucasus area on his release, he was repeatedly arrested between 1902 and 1913, but always managed to escape. In 1912, by then in St Petersburg, he became one of the first editors of the revolutionary newspaper *Pravda*. He was again arrested in 1913 and exiled to Siberia for life, but was released under amnesty after the February Revolution of 1917. He rapidly emerged as a leading Bolshevik, and surrounded himself with politicians upon whose loyalty he could count. After the October Revolution he became People's Commissar for Nationalities in the Soviet government, and in 1922 he was appointed General Secretary of the Party Central Committee, a post he held until his death.

After the death of Lenin in 1924 he set about the systematic elimination of every possible rival and embarked on a savage purge of the higher military echelons, precipitating a terror that reached its peak in 1937–8 and robbed the Soviet Army of many of its most talented commanders, with disastrous results when the Germans invaded in 1941. His series of five-year plans, inaugurated in 1928 and designed to transform Soviet industry and agriculture, were equally disastrous; the attempts to 'collectivize' Russian agriculture resulted only in massive crop failures and the deaths of millions through famine. This period saw the emergence of a repressive, authoritarian state, propped up by the enormous power of the secret police.

In August 1939 Stalin signed a non-aggression pact with Nazi Germany, leaving the way clear for the Germans to invade Poland from the west and for the Russians to occupy the eastern part. When the Germans attacked Russia in June 1941, making staggering progress initially, Stalin lost little time in assuming personal command of all military operations, displaying forceful leadership and a brutal indifference to the suffering of the Russian people. Yet the people, with their ancient love of the Rodina, the Motherland, responded to his exhortations and produced magnificent displays of stubborn courage, particularly during the siege of Leningrad and at Stalingrad. At the same time, Stalin was supported by a hard core of excellent military commanders such as Zhukov, Chuikov and Koniev.

Stalin was a talented diplomat, and at the various conferences during and after World War II he won considerable concessions, especially from America's ailing President Roosevelt, which ensured Soviet domination of large areas of eastern Europe and precipitated the Cold War. At home, his repressions and persecutions were resumed and continued until his death in 1953. Three years later, his regime was denounced by Russia's new leader, Nikita Khrushchev, who inaugurated a series of de-Stalinization programmes.

Josef Stalin ran his Soviet regime with brutal repression. Its trappings were soon swept away after his death.

General Joseph Warren Stilwell
US Army

Not noted for his powers of diplomacy in later life, particularly when it came to dealing with his superiors, Joseph Warren Stilwell was born on 19 March 1883. He attended the US Military Academy, West Point, from 1900 to 1904, excelling at track events and basketball, and served in the Philippines as a 2nd lieutenant before returning to West Point as a languages and sports instructor. During World War I he fought at St-Mihiel and Verdun, and by the end of hostilities he had risen to the rank of colonel. This was a temporary rank, however, and in 1919 he dropped back to captain. It took him ten years to become a colonel again; during most of that time he had served in China, and was fluent in the various Chinese dialects. He was then assigned to head the tactical section at the Infantry School, Fort Benning, and it was during his time there that he acquired the nickname 'Vinegar Joe', the result of a rather unkind caricature drawn by a student.

When America entered World War II, Stilwell's expertise in China and its ways made him the ideal choice for adviser, and later Chief of Staff, to General Chiang Kai-shek, the Nationalist leader. In 1942, as the Japanese advanced through Burma, the Chinese 5th Army, under Stilwell's direction, marched south and fought a spirited battle at Toungoo. Although prickly and temperamental, Stilwell was not without military talent, and wielded his Chinese forces effectively, but without air cover

there was little they could achieve, and they were forced to retreat back to China. Stilwell was also in command of all American forces in the China–Burma–India theatre, which caused problems for Lord Louis Mountbatten, who became Stilwell's superior when he arrived to take over as Supreme Commander. One of Mountbatten's first acts was to integrate the Allied air forces under a single commander, which greatly enhanced their efficiency.

Stilwell's outspokenness was his undoing. Disagreements between Chiang Kai-shek and his fiery Chief of Staff developed into an open breach, and in October 1944 Stilwell was recalled to the United States at Chiang's insistence. At least one person regretted his departure, and that was Field Marshal Sir William Slim, commander of the Fourteenth Army, who later commented: 'In Fourteenth Army and, I think, throughout the British forces our sympathies were with Stilwell – unlike the American 14th Air Force who demonstratively rejoiced at his downfall . . . There was no one whom I would rather have had commanding the Chinese army that was to advance with mine. Under Stilwell, it *would* advance. We saw him go with regret, and he took with him our admiration as a fighting soldier.'

In 1945, he was made Chief of Army Ground Forces, and commanded the US 10th Army on Okinawa. In October 1946, only a few months after his retirement, General 'Vinegar Joe' Stilwell died from cancer.

General Joseph 'Vinegar Joe' Stilwell performed miracles in welding the Chinese Army into an effective fighting force. (National Archives)

General Kurt Student
German Army

General Kurt Student, the architect of Germany's airborne forces. (Bundesarchiv)

given command of the Flight Test Centre at Rechlin, with the rank of Oberst.

Early in 1938 he was appointed to command the newly formed 7th Fliegerdivision, with the task of organizing Germany's embryo airborne forces. He personally led the division during the airborne assault on Holland and Belgium in May 1940, but on 14 May, while negotiating a cease-fire in Rotterdam, he was accidentally shot in the head by a German soldier, a mishap that put him out of action for several months. He returned to active service in January 1941, when he was promoted General and awarded the Knight's Cross. In the spring of 1941 he planned and executed Operation Merkur, the airborne invasion of Crete; it began on 20 May and eventually succeeded, but at terrible cost; nearly a quarter of the invasion force was killed. It was the last time that German paratroops were used in their intended role. Although their numbers were increased, from now on they would fight as ground troops in Sicily, Italy, Normandy and the Ardennes.

In September 1943, mainly as a reward for planning the operation in which the Italian dictator Mussolini was rescued by glider troops under Otto Skorzeny, Student was awarded the Oak Leaves to his Knight's Cross, and

The man who would rise to fame as the commander of Germany's airborne forces in World War II, Kurt Arthur Benno Student, was born at Birkhonz, Germany, on 12 May 1890. At the age of 11 he entered a military school, and in 1910 he joined a Prussian infantry battalion. Shortly after the outbreak of World War I, as a Leutnant, he transferred to the German Flying Corps and trained as a fighter pilot, being seriously wounded in 1917. After the war, returning to the infantry, he became involved with the formation of the clandestine Luftwaffe, and when the Nazis came to power he was appointed Director of Technical Training Schools under Hermann Goering. In 1935, with the existence of the Luftwaffe out in the open, he was

in July 1944 he was given command of the 1st Paratroop Army, rising to command Army Group H as a Generaloberst at the end of the year. He was soon replaced, however, and reverted to the command of the 1st Paratroop Army, his last command of the war. In April 1945 he was captured by British forces in northern Germany. Tried as a war criminal, he was sentenced to five years' imprisonment, but served only two.

General Kurt Student died in Lemgo, West Germany, on 1 July 1978. It may be said that he made his mark on World War II by default; had he elected to invade the vital island of Malta instead of Crete, control of the Mediterranean would almost certainly have passed to the Germans.

Born in Keytesville, Missouri, on 26 August 1901, Maxwell Davenport Taylor graduated from West Point in 1922 and subsequently served in Hawaii with the 3rd Engineers. He spent much of the inter-war years studying languages, becoming proficient in French, Spanish and Japanese. He graduated from the Army War College in 1940 and was promoted major; in 1940–41 he commanded the 12th Field Artillery Battalion, and in December 1941 he became a lieutenant-colonel. By the end of 1942 he was a brigadier-general, and Chief of Staff to the 82nd Airborne Division. He accompanied the division to Sicily and Italy in 1943, and was cited for bravery for crossing enemy lines to confer with Italian resistance leaders on the possibility of seizing airfields near Rome.

In May 1944 Taylor received temporary promotion to major-general and was given command of the 101st Airborne Division, which had formed on 15 August 1942 from an element of the 82nd Airborne Division, remaining in the USA until August 1943, and which he subsequently commanded during the invasion of Normandy and the campaign in north-west Europe. In September 1944 the division dropped into Holland to secure the strategic river crossings north of Eindhoven, and in December it was heavily involved in the German offensive in the Ardennes, holding up the enemy advance by its gallant defence at Bastogne, where it was commanded by Taylor's deputy, General McAuliffe (who uttered the famous word 'Nuts!' in reply to a German surrender demand).

In 1949 General Taylor was Chief of Staff of the European Command, and in 1953 he took command of the US Eighth Army in the final phase of the war in Korea. In 1954–5 he commanded United States Forces, Far East, and in 1955 was appointed head of the United Nations Command. From 1955 to 1959 he was Chief of Staff of the United States Army, and like his airborne forces colleague General Gavin he

General Maxwell D. Taylor

opposed the doctrine of massive nuclear retaliation, favouring the flexible response policy that was later adopted by NATO.

General Taylor retired from active service in July 1959, but was recalled as Chairman of the Joint Chiefs of Staff in 1962. He was Ambassador to South Vietnam in 1964–5 and later held a number of advisory posts in the fields of intelligence and defence.

General Maxwell Taylor died in Washington, DC, on 19 April 1987.

Marshal of the Royal Air Force Lord Tedder
Royal Air Force

Arthur Tedder was one of the most able of the Allied air commanders, and was Eisenhower's deputy at the time of D-Day. (National Archives)

The son of a civil servant, Arthur William Tedder was born at Glenguin, Scotland, in July 1890. Educated at Magdalene College, Cambridge, he was awarded the Prince Consort Prize for History in 1912, for an essay on the Royal Navy of the Restoration. On the outbreak of World War I he was commissioned into the Dorsetshire Regiment, but in 1916 transferred to the Royal Flying Corps, and at the end of the conflict he was in command of No. 70 Squadron, flying Sopwith Camel fighters. Tedder's post-war appointments included commander of the Air Armament School (1934–6), Director of Training at the Air Ministry (1936–8) and, as an air vice-marshal, Director-General of Research and Development, a post he filled from 1938 to 1940. In December that year he was posted to the Middle East as deputy to Air Marshal Arthur Longmore, and on 1 June 1941, with Longmore's departure, he was appointed Air Officer Commanding-in-Chief, Middle East.

In the months that followed, with consummate skill, Tedder – who assumed command at a time of great crisis, with the withdrawal from Greece in progress, Rommel on the offensive and the island of Malta under intense bombardment – threw his energies into land–air co-operation, and forged the instrument that was to play such a vital part in Rommel's defeat, the Desert Air Force. In 1943, after the Axis defeat in Tunisia, he was appointed commander-in-chief of the Mediterranean Air Command, in which capacity he worked closely with General Eisenhower and was responsible for land–air co-ordination during the invasion of Sicily and Italy. In 1944 he was appointed Deputy Supreme Allied Commander under Eisenhower in preparing Operation Overlord, planning the preparatory bombing operations and tactical air support during and after the Normandy landings.

In May 1945 Tedder signed the instrument of surrender of the German forces on Eisenhower's behalf. In 1946 he became Chief of the Air Staff, and was elevated to the peerage. He retired from the RAF in 1950, and was chairman of the British Joint Services Commission before becoming Chancellor of Cambridge University.

Marshal of the Royal Air Force Lord Tedder died in Surrey on 3 June 1967.

Air Marshal Tedder and General Montgomery discussing aspects of air–ground co-operation in the desert. (IWM)

Marshal Tito
Yugoslav Partisan Leader

A blacksmith's son, Tito was born Josip Broz in 1892 at Kumrovec, Austria-Hungary (later Croatia). The nickname Tito, which literally means 'This-That', was acquired later because of his habit of issuing rapid-fire orders. He fought with the Imperial Austro-Hungarian Army during World War I, being captured by the Russians, and served with the Bolshevik Army during the Russian Civil War (1918–20), afterwards returning to his native Croatia to become a leading organizer of labour unions. His activities caused him to be imprisoned as a political agitator from 1929 to 1934, but in 1937 he was assigned the task of organizing the Yugoslav Communist Party. In 1941, he emerged as leader of guerrilla resistance to the occupying Axis powers, despite the support which the Yugoslav government in exile gave to Mihailovic, the Serbian resistance leader.

Tito's success as a guerrilla leader may be attributed to his lightning tactics, his dynamic personality, his stamina and, above all, his ruthlessness in the cause of Communism and Yugoslav independence. During his leadership of the partisans he received little aid from the USSR, but from 1944, when air bases became available in Italy, a constant flow of air-dropped material was sent by the Allies. The British, in particular, were quick to appreciate the potential value of the partisan movement, and established a military mission in Yugoslavia in 1943. Tito was proclaimed marshal in December 1943, and in 1944 his partisans worked with the Red Army in driving the Germans out of Yugoslavia. Tito then became the dominant figure in the Federal People's Republic of Yugoslavia. The

A man of immense inner strength, Marshal Tito refused to be bullied by the Soviet leadership.

monarchy was abolished, Mihailovic was summarily executed and other opposition figures, notably the Archbishop of Zagreb, were imprisoned. Tito, thereafter virtual dictator of Yugoslavia, co-operated with the USSR but frequently took an independent line, trading with both East and West. His intransigence led to Yugoslavia being expelled from the Comintern, the economic union of the Soviet bloc. He was repeatedly re-elected President of Yugoslavia, and in 1963 he was granted the appointment for life. He died in Ljubljana on 4 May 1980, and in the decade that followed the various states that made up Yugoslavia slid relentlessly towards anarchy.

Croatian volunteers, opponents of Tito, in conversation with German officers. (Bundesarchiv)

Harry S. Truman
US President

President Harry S. Truman had the awesome responsibility of authorizing the atomic bomb attacks on Japan. (National Archives)

Harry S. Truman, the 33rd President of the United States, was born in Lamar, Missouri, in 1884, and grew up in Independence as a member of a farming family. Unable to attend college because of his family's poverty, he joined the US Army and served as an artillery captain on the Western Front in World War I. On his return he married Elizabeth Virginia Wallace, and opened a haberdashery in Kansas City. Turning to politics, he became active in the Democratic Party, and in 1922 he was elected a judge of the Jackson County Court (an administrative position). He became a Senator in 1934, and by 1940 he had become a renowned figure in American politics for his chairmanship of the Senate War Investigating Committee, which revealed gross instances of fraud in the national defence budget. Truman was nominated as Vice-President in 1944 and was duly elected in President Franklin D. Roosevelt's shadow. He scarcely saw the President, and knew nothing about key wartime projects such as the development of the atomic bomb, and when he became President on 12 April 1945, after Roosevelt's sudden death, he declared that he felt as though the moon, the planets and all the stars had fallen on him.

As President, Truman soon showed that he was very much his own master, and fully capable of independent decision. When told that the first atomic device had been successfully tested, he immediately authorized its use as a military weapon against Japan, with the object of bringing the war to a swift end and saving countless Allied and enemy lives. After the destruction of Hiroshima and Nagasaki, Japan's surrender quickly followed.

One of Truman's most important post-war actions was to implement a 21-point plan aimed at improving his country's standard of living, an important aspect of which was slum clearance. It was Truman who stood firm when the Russians blockaded Berlin in 1948–9, authorizing the massive airlift that saved the city, and in 1949 he presided over the foundation of the North Atlantic Treaty Organization, designed to preserve the West against Soviet aggression. He also stood firm during the Korean War, when he was forced to make some unpleasant decisions, mostly to do with General Douglas MacArthur, whose desire to use nuclear weapons against Chinese troop concentrations had to be firmly overruled.

In 1953 Truman was succeeded as US President by General Dwight D. Eisenhower, and went into retirement. He died on 26 December 1972, after a long battle against cancer.

Admiral Richmond K. Turner
US Navy

Admiral Richmond K. Turner's development of amphibious operations made an enormous contribution to Allied victory.
(National Archives)

Richmond Kelly Turner was born in Portland, Oregon, on 27 May 1885. In 1904 he entered the US Naval Academy, graduating in 1908, and after service on small ships he served in battleships from 1916 to 1919. In the 1920s he specialized mainly in gunnery, but took flight training in 1927, and in the following decade he undertook several aviation-related assignments, including one as Executive Officer of the aircraft-carrier USS *Saratoga*. In 1939, as commander of the heavy cruiser *Astoria*, he went on a diplomatic mission to Japan. In 1941, as Director of the War Plans Division, US Navy, he reached the rank of rear-admiral. From December 1941 to June 1942 he was Assistant Chief of Staff to the Commander-in-Chief, US Fleet, and was then sent to the Pacific to take command of the South Pacific Force's Amphibious Force – one of the most important and demanding assignments of World War II.

Over the next three years, Turner developed the perilous art of ship-to-shore landings under fire, beginning with the landing on Guadalcanal in August 1942 – the first major American amphibious operation of the war against a hostile coast, when the US 1st Marine Division went ashore from fifteen transport vessels. During the weeks that followed, Turner directed the passage of the vital reinforcement convoys that fought their way through to the island, enabling the US troops to consolidate their position until the Japanese were finally forced to withdraw. In June 1943 Turner commanded Task Force 31, which landed troops on Rendova in the central Solomons, and in November he led Task Force 52 in operations against the Gilbert Islands. This was followed, in January 1944, by a landing on Kwajalein Atoll, and in June 1944 Turner, now a vice-admiral, commanded Task Force 52, which landed the V Amphibious Corps on Saipan. In February 1945 Turner's ships began landing V Amphibious Corps on Iwo Jima, precipitating one of the bloodiest battles of the Pacific war, and in April he directed Operation Iceberg, the landings on Okinawa. Three months later, Admiral Turner was planning what was to be the most massive amphibious operation of the war – the assault on Japan itself. Fortunately, this undertaking, which would have resulted in an enormous loss of life, was made unnecessary by the dropping of the atomic bombs.

After the war, Admiral Turner served on the Navy Department's General Board and was US Naval representative on the United Nations Military Staff Committee. He retired in 1947, and died in Monterey, California, on 12 February 1961.

Major-General Robert E. Urquhart
British Army

For an airborne forces' commander, Major-General Robert 'Roy' Urquhart appeared to have singularly few qualifications. For one thing, he was too old to qualify as a paratrooper; for another, he was prone to airsickness. But there was no doubt at all about his prowess as a fighting soldier. As an officer with the 51st Highland Division, he had taken part in many savage battles across North Africa, on Sicily and in Italy. Then, early in 1944, he was unexpectedly chosen to command the British 1st Airborne Division, whose previous commander, General Eric Down, had been transferred to India to form new airborne units there.

The 1st Airborne Division did not take part in the Normandy invasion of June 1944, but in a ten-week period that followed it stood by to take part in sixteen planned drops on key points behind enemy lines, none of which in fact took place. Then came September 1944, and the biggest airborne operation ever mounted: Operation Market Garden, in which the 1st Allied Airborne Army, comprising the British 1st Airborne Division and the US 82nd and 101st Airborne Divisions, together with glider-borne forces, were to capture strategic bridges in Holland. The 1st Airborne Division's objective was the bridge at Arnhem, and the fighting there soon took a disastrous turn for the British, who encountered

Major-General Robert 'Roy' Urquhart outside his HQ at the Hartenstein Hotel, Arnhem, September 1944. (IWM)

fierce resistance from two Panzer divisions that were regrouping in the area. The division made its drop on 17 September, and the next day the confused nature of the fighting separated Urquhart from his divisional HQ, forcing him to take refuge in a house until the following morning. Together with one of his subordinate commanders, Brigadier Lathbury, Urquhart fought his way to safety with the help of some Dutch civilians, and regained his HQ, but by that time the Germans were gaining control of the situation. By 21 September, all hope that the 1st Airborne Division might still be capable of fulfilling its original mission had vanished, and Urquhart ordered a defensive perimeter to be set up at Oosterbeek, where he hoped his troops might hold on until the arrival of General Brian Horrocks's XXX Corps. But the advance of XXX Corps had been held up, and Urquhart was left with no choice but to order the remnants of his division to escape across the Rhine.

Urquhart's superior at Arnhem was Lieutenant-General F.A.H. Browning DSO, who was said to have made the comment that the Allies had gone a 'bridge too far'.

Marshal Kliment Yefremovich Voroshilov
Soviet Army

Born in 1881, the son of a railway worker, Kliment Voroshilov joined the Communist Party in 1903 and was an extremely active member prior to World War I, first meeting Lenin in 1906. He took part in the February Revolution of 1917, and helped to form Red Guard units before the October Revolution. Appointed Commissar for Petrograd in November 1917, he organized the Lugansk Detachment which defended Kharkov against German forces early in 1918. In 1919 he commanded the 14th Army, and in 1919–21 he was a member of the general staff of the 1st Cavalry Army under Budenny. From 1921 to 1924 he commanded the Caucasus Military District, mopping up bands of guerrillas who remained loyal to the now deceased Tsar, and later he became the People's Commissar for Naval and Military Affairs. In 1934 he was appointed People's Commissar for Defence, and in the following year he was one of the first five officers to become Marshals of the Soviet Union. Only he and one other, Budenny – both, significantly, members of the old Bolshevik cavalry élite – would survive the purges of the late 1930s.

Voroshilov made an important contribution to modernizing the Red Army and equipping it to fight a war of manoeuvre, but the German attack of June 1941 showed how ill prepared the Russian forces still were. By this time Voroshilov was a member of the State Defence Committee (GKO) and the Stavka. In 1942 he was given the task of organizing partisan forces, briefing commanders personally before their insertion behind German lines. In January 1943 he was Stavka co-ordinator of the Leningrad and Volkhov Fronts during the Russian offensive that raised the siege of Leningrad, and in 1943 he supervised the naval and military operations that led to the recapture of the Crimea. After the war he was president of the Soviet Control Commission in Hungary for two years, and on the death of Stalin in 1953 he was elected to the presidency of the Soviet Union. His days of power came to an abrupt end in 1960, when Premier Khrushchev forced him to resign. In 1966, following Khrushchev's departure, he was once more elected to the Central Committee, but died in 1969.

Marshal Voroshilov rose to supreme power under Stalin's regime, but was dismissed by Nikita Khrushchev.

Field Marshal Lord Wavell
British Army

Field Marshal Wavell (right), with General Auchinleck, shortly after the latter had assumed command in the Middle East. (IWM)

Field Marshal Sir Archibald Percival, Lord Wavell, was born in Colchester, Essex, on 5 May 1883, the son of Major-General A.G. Wavell CBE. Educated at Winchester College, he entered the Royal Military College at Sandhurst and was commissioned into the 42nd Highland Regiment (the Black Watch) in 1901, serving in the South African Boer War and later on India's troubled North-West Frontier. He was wounded in World War I and awarded the Military Cross. Post-war service brought him a wide variety of commands and rapid promotion: by 1933 he was a major-general, and this was followed by promotion to lieutenant-general five years later. In 1939 he was appointed Commander-in-Chief, Middle East, and with only relatively weak forces at his disposal he was faced with the daunting task of building a barrier to Axis expansion across a vast tract of territory covering many lands and incorporating many different peoples.

He rose to it magnificently. During his tenure as C-in-C the Italian East African Empire was destroyed, General Graziani's army in Cyrenaica was obliterated, and German-inspired anti-British revolts in the oil-rich lands of the Near East were crushed. All these achievements, however, were negated by Churchill's insistence on diverting a substantial proportion of Wavell's scant resources to supporting the doomed campaign in Greece: the ejection of British forces from the Balkans was followed rapidly by the loss of Crete and the reconquest of Cyrenaica by Rommel.

In November 1941 Churchill, impatient at Wavell's delay in opening a new offensive, transferred him to the position of Commander-in-Chief, India. In January 1942 he was appointed Supreme Commander, South-West Pacific ABDA (American, British, Dutch, Australian) Command, a post he held until March, when he resigned. By that time, ABDA no longer existed as a cohesive command, the Japanese having overrun most of the area it was supposed to control. Wavell continued to hold the post of C-in-C India during the rest of 1942, a period that saw the longest fighting retreat in the history of the British Army, the withdrawal through Burma. In December 1942 his troops launched a limited offensive in the Arakan, on the India–Burma frontier, but made no headway.

In January 1943, Wavell was made a field marshal and became Viscount Wavell of Cyrenaica. He was appointed Viceroy and Governor-General of India, a post he held until 1947. He died on 24 May 1950.

General Maxime Weygand
French Army

General Maxime Weygand arriving in France to take command of the Allied armies, June 1940. (author's collection)

Born in Brussels on 21 January 1867, Maxime Weygand entered the French Military College at St-Cyr in 1885 and embarked on a brilliant military career. Rising steadily in rank, he was appointed chief of staff to General Foch in October 1914. He participated in the Ypres and Yser operations in October–December 1914, in Artois in 1915, and on the Somme in 1916. For a time in the winter of 1917–18 he was France's representative on the Versailles war council, but rejoined Foch in March 1918. His work in the critical battles of March–October that year was exceedingly brilliant, although he received less recognition for it than he deserved.

In 1920 he travelled to Poland to advise the embryo Polish Army in its war against the Russians. Two years after his return he was appointed high commissioner in Syria, and in 1931 he was made commander-in-chief of the French Army. In 1939, after four years of retirement, he was recalled to duty and sent back to Syria as military commander. He was still there on 10 May 1940, when the

Germans launched their offensive against France and the Low Countries. On 18 May he was in Cairo, conferring with General Wavell, when an urgent signal arrived from French Premier Paul Reynaud, summoning him to Paris. The next day, he was informed that he was to assume command of all French forces.

He was faced with an impossible task. The Germans had just broken through and were racing for the English Channel, driving a wedge between the Allied armies. Weygand set up a new line of defence south of the Somme and conducted a valiant defence, but his troops were weary and dispirited and they could not contain the German armoured thrusts. After the Franco-German armistice of June 1940, Weygand served in the Vichy government as Minister of Defence, later becoming Governor-General of Algeria. In 1942 he was taken as a hostage by the Germans and imprisoned near Salzburg, being liberated by the Americans in 1945. He was briefly indicted as a collaborator, but was exonerated in 1948. He died in 1964.

Major-General Charles Orde Wingate
British Army

Once described by General Sir William Slim, commander of the Fourteenth Army in Burma, as a 'strange, excitable, moody creature, but he had a fire in him . . . he could ignite other men', Orde Wingate was born at Naini Tal, India, on 26 February 1903, the son of an army officer. His parents were members of the deeply religious Plymouth Brethren sect, a fact that may have had much to do with the way Wingate's character was subsequently shaped. Educated at Charterhouse and Woolwich, he graduated in 1923 and was commissioned into the Royal Artillery. After a period at the School of Oriental Studies, London, he served for five years in the Sudan Defence Force before joining the British intelligence staff in Palestine in 1936 as a captain. There, he organized counter-terrorist operations against Arab dissidents, who were attacking both Jews and British troops. During this period, he developed an intense passion for the Zionist cause, so much so that in 1939 the British succumbed to Arab pressure and transferred him to the Middle East Command, under General Wavell.

Unhappy in his personal life, Orde Wingate possessed great personal courage, and was cast in the same mould as Lawrence of Arabia. (National Archives)

Upon Italy's entry into the war Wavell gave Wingate the task of conducting raiding operations into Abyssinia, for which purpose he formed a special unit known as Gideon Force. A manic depressive, he suffered a severe breakdown and was hospitalized for several months, during which time he tried to commit suicide. Afterwards, he joined Wavell in India, where he proposed the formation of long-range penetration groups to operate behind the Japanese lines in Burma. In February 1943 he launched the first Chindit expedition, sending 3,000 men into Burma on a five-month operation from which 2,000 returned, and of those 600 were no longer fit to fight. Nevertheless, Winston Churchill approved of the scheme, and later in 1943 Wingate was promoted major-general and given six brigades of the 3rd Indian Division. In February 1944 a large Chindit force was infiltrated by gliders to an airstrip 200 miles inside Japanese territory and caused considerable disruption, but Wingate never lived to witness its success. On 24 March 1944, he was killed when the USAAF C-46 in which he was flying crashed in India.

The remains of Major-General Orde Wingate DSO and two Bars today lie in Arlington National Cemetery, alongside those of nine Americans who were also killed in the accident.

Chindits embarking on a Dakota transport aircraft. (author's collection)

Admiral Isoroku Yamamoto
Japanese Navy

Isoroku Yamamoto was born in 1884. He was an adopted child, his original family name being Takano. He graduated from the Japanese Naval Academy in 1904, and in the following year he saw action in the naval battle at Tsushima during the Russo-Japanese war, losing two fingers. He attended the Naval War College and then went to the United States to study at Harvard. Later, as a captain, he served as Naval Attaché to the United States from 1925 to 1927; he therefore knew the Americans well, and was fluent in English.

After serving in a number of posts – many of them connected with naval aviation – in the 1930s, he was appointed Commander-in-Chief of the Japanese Combined Fleet in 1939, and in 1940 he made a thorough study of the attack on Taranto naval base by British carrier aircraft, which resulted in the crippling of major components of the Italian fleet. This lesson he used to good advantage when, on a much larger scale, he planned the attack on Pearl Harbor in December 1941. Yamamoto was responsible for planning most naval operations during this period, although his plan to eliminate America's remaining naval power by launching an attack on Midway Island in June 1942 went badly wrong when American naval aircraft sank the fleet carriers *Akagi*, *Kaga*, *Hiryu* and *Soryu*, effectively eliminating Japan's naval strike force. Despite this adverse outcome Yamamoto remained in command during the ensuing campaign for the possession of Guadalcanal in the Solomons, which further depleted Japan's naval resources.

On 18 April 1943, the Americans, having broken the Japanese naval code, learned that Yamamoto was conducting a tour of Japanese naval bases in the Bougainville area, and despatched sixteen Lockheed P-38 Lightnings from Henderson Field, Guadalcanal, to intercept the aircraft carrying the admiral. The Mitsubishi G4M 'Betty' bomber was intercepted after a 435-mile (700 km) overwater flight and shot down into the jungle, all on board being killed. The death of Yamamoto, who was posthumously promoted to the rank of Admiral of the Fleet, had a profound effect on the Japanese conduct of the war in the Pacific, and on Japanese morale in general.

Isoroku Yamamoto pictured on the bridge of his flagship.
(author's collection)

The remains of Admiral Yamamoto's 'Betty' bomber in the jungle where it was shot down. (author's collection)

General Tomoyuki Yamashita
Japanese Army

Tomoyuki Yamashita, the 'Tiger of Malaya', pictured in captivity after his surrender to the Allies. (via J. R. Cavanagh)

Born in 1883, Tomoyuki Yamashita graduated with honours from the Hiroshima Military Academy in 1908 and was commissioned into the infantry. In the 1920s he travelled widely on military assignments; these included the posts of military attaché in Vienna and Budapest. In 1930–31 he was appointed to command the 3rd Infantry Regiment; this was followed by two staff appointments, first as head of the Army Affairs Section in the War Ministry, and then as chief of military research in the same location. In 1936 he was assigned to the command of the 40th Brigade in Korea, in 1937 he was commanding the China Mixed Brigade, and in 1939 he was chief of staff of the Northern China Area Army. The years 1939–40 saw him commanding the 4th Division in Manchuria during the Sino-Japanese war, and in 1940–1 he was head of Japanese Army Aviation, an appointment that gave him a close insight into the essential points of air-ground co-operation. In the latter months of 1941 he headed a Japanese military mission that travelled to Berlin and Rome.

On his return he was appointed commander of the Japanese 25th Army for the invasion of Malaya. A well-planned and tactically inspired campaign was crowned between 8 and 15 February 1942, when his forces captured the island fortress of Singapore, together with thousands of Allied prisoners, many of whom were to die under the brutal regime of Japanese prison camps.

At the close of the successful campaigns in Malaya and the Dutch East Indies Yamashita returned to Manchuria to command the 1st Area Army, a post he held until 1944, when he was transferred to become General Officer Commanding the 14th Area Army in the Philippines. He commanded the Japanese forces in the area during their unsuccessful defence of the Philippines against the invading Americans, who had the advantage after the virtual elimination of Japanese naval and air power at the Battle of Leyte Gulf in October 1944. Nevertheless, the Japanese continued to put up a fanatical resistance in isolated pockets, and it was not until September 1945 that Yamashita surrendered the Philippines. He was later put on trial to answer for the atrocities committed by the troops under his command, condemned as a war criminal, and hanged in 1946.

General Andrei I. Yeremenko
Soviet Army

Born in 1892, Andrei Yeremenko was conscripted into the Imperial Russian Army in World War I and reached the rank of corporal before the Army collapsed in chaos following the October Revolution. Joining the Red Army, he took part in the latter's campaign against the Poles in 1920, in which the Russians were decisively defeated. In 1941 he was in command of an army in the Far East, but was urgently summoned to Moscow by Stalin when the Germans invaded and given command of the Bryansk sector of the Western Front, whose overall commander was the People's Commissar for Defence, Marshal Timoshenko. The situation was desperate, but Yeremenko, through sheer force of personality, got every serviceable aircraft into the air to attack the advancing Panzer columns. Losses were appalling: by 1 July no more than 120 aircraft remained on the Western Front's air strength, and the Front's air commander, General D.G. Pavlov, had committed suicide.

Yeremenko organized air reinforcements and then counter-attacked with a tank group equipped with the new T-34 and KV-1 models, whose armour could not be penetrated by German anti-tank shells. The action was temporarily successful, throwing back the Germans at the very gates of Moscow and badly disrupting the timetable of Operation Barbarossa, whose principal objectives were not achieved before the onset of winter. Command of the Western Front subsequently devolved upon Marshal Georgi Zhukov, who organized Moscow's defences and planned subsequent counter-attacks. August 1941 was a critical month, and Yeremenko, writing in his memoirs, later recalled that : 'The Frontal Air Force, utilizing every flying day, inflicted great losses on the enemy. On August 30 and 31 alone, around 1,500 sorties were flown, 4,000 bombs were dropped, more than 100 tanks and 20 armoured vehicles were destroyed, a fuel dump was blown up, and 55 aircraft were destroyed.'

Yeremenko was later involved in the fighting before Moscow, where he was wounded, and later at Stalingrad. In May 1945 his troops liberated Prague. He possessed outstanding tactical skills, but was overshadowed by Marshal Zhukov and given little opportunity to exercise his talents as a strategist. He died in retirement in 1970.

Although an outstanding tactician, particularly in armoured manoeuvre, Andrei Yeremenko was always overshadowed by Marshal Zhukov. (via J. R. Cavanagh)

Marshal Georgi Konstantinovich Zhukov
Soviet Army

Born in 1896, Georgi K. Zhukov was the son of a village cobbler, and was serving his apprenticeship to a Moscow furrier when he was conscripted into the Russian Army in 1915. Assigned to the cavalry, he joined the Red Army when Russia became torn by civil war, serving as a company and squadron commander. In 1923 he was appointed to command the 39th Buzuluk Cavalry Regiment, and in 1930, following completion of the Cavalry Higher Command course, he was given command of the 2nd Cavalry Brigade. Other commands in the 1930s included the 4th Cavalry Division and the 3rd and 6th Cavalry Corps, culminating, in the summer of 1939, in the 1st Army Group, created to repel the Japanese incursion into Mongolia. Zhukov, now a lieutenant-general, won a decisive victory at Khalkin Gol and was made a Hero of the Soviet Union.

Zhukov, unlike so many others, escaped Stalin's notorious purges of the late 1930s, which decimated the Red Army's leadership. Appointed to the rank of Army (full) general, he was given command of the Kiev Military District, and between January and July 1941 he was Chief of the General Staff. On 23 June 1941 he was made a member of the Stavka (Supreme High Command), in which capacity he helped organize Russia's early counter-offensives against the Germans. From 12 September he conducted a masterly defence at Leningrad, effectively halting the Germans, and in October he moved to the Moscow Front to organize the capital's defences and then launch a counter-attack with reserve forces from Siberia.

In 1942–3 Zhukov co-ordinated the actions of several fronts at Stalingrad, Leningrad, Kursk and the Dnieper. He was promoted a Marshal of the Soviet Union in 1943, and from March to May 1944 he commanded the 1st Ukrainian Front, and that summer he co-ordinated the actions of the 1st and 2nd Byelorussian Fronts in the massive strategic offensive operation that would end in the heart of Germany. From November 1944 to May 1945 he commanded the 1st Byelorussian Front in the

The greatest of all Russian generals, Georgi Zhukov fell out of favour when Nikita Khrushchev assumed power. (via J. R. Cavanagh)

Vistula-Oder and Berlin operations, and on 8 May 1945 he was the first of the Allied commanders to sign the instrument of surrender at Karlshorst, outside Berlin.

Zhukov remained in command of the Soviet Group of Forces, Germany, until June 1946, when he was given command of the Odessa and Ural Military Districts, a move doubtless calculated by Stalin to remove the popular soldier from the public eye. After the death of Stalin he became a First Deputy Minister, and was nominated for a seat on the Central Committee. He actively assisted Nikita Khrushchev's rise to power, only to be dismissed by the latter in 1957 for 'fostering a personal cult' and attempting to remove the armed forces from Communist Party control.

Marshal Georgi K. Zhukov died in 1974.

Index

References to Commanders and Heroes are in addition to those shown in Contents.